Love and Liberty

L4407

Love and Liberty

FAITH AND UNITY IN A
POSTMODERN AGE

JOHN GLADWIN

DARTON · LONGMAN + TODD

First published in 1998 by
Darton, Longman and Todd Ltd
1 Spencer Court
140–142 Wandsworth High Street
London SW18 4JJ

ISBN 0–232–52247–2

A catalogue record for this book is available from the British Library.

Designed by Sandie Boccacci
Phototypeset in 10¼/13½pt Times by Intype
Printed and bound in Great Britain by
Redwood Books, Trowbridge, Wiltshire

Contents

Preface

This book has been in my heart for a long time. The opportunities we have for making something good out of the changing and multi-faceted society of our times are enormous. Yet, the Church still seems to view the emerging world with a certain amount of both fear and bewilderment. Every age has helped us experience the eternal meaning of the life and being of God in fresh and creative ways. Ours is no exception. At the heart of this book is a desire to think anew about God. Then to allow that meditation to interplay with the cultural shifts of a postmodern world.

In the writing of this book I owe much to many. To my colleagues over many years and in different settings of ministry my thanks for the stimulation of shared work and for their own honest wrestling with the faith today. Especial thanks to my colleagues in the team who work with me in Guildford who took on extra responsibility during my study leave in 1997. This gave me the space to write and to get out what was inside my life. I hope what is here will encourage them in the wonderful things they bring to the Church and world today.

My good friend Tim Dean took time amidst all the demands of his own professional life with the BBC to read early drafts and apply the rigour of his mind to my theme. I am grateful for his attention to both the broad impact and to the detail. I am responsible for the outcome. He helped me to make a theme into a book. Thank you!

I dedicate this book to my wife Lydia whose encouragement gave me the confidence to do the task. She has supported me with patience and with wise and enabling thought throughout the months I have been making sense of the theme. Her enjoyment of life in the wider world and the contribution she makes to so many circles of our modern life encourage me to believe that there are many who will warm to the thesis of love working for human liberty.

JOHN GLADWIN
Lent, 1998

Introduction

The parable of the twentieth century

John Updike has written a parable for our century. In *In the Beauty of the Lilies* he takes us through the changing visions of the last century. Interestingly the story begins with the life of a Presbyterian minister who loses his faith and abandons the ministry. It ends close to our own time a couple of generations later in the world of alternative and apocalyptic culture and the terrible carnage as the FBI destroy this sectarian community in a massive attack. In between it passes through the materialism and secularism of this century.

> At the moment when Mary Pickford fainted, the Reverend Clarence Arthur Wilmot, down in the parsonage of the Fourth Presbyterian Church at the corner of Straight Street and Broadway, felt the last particles of his faith leave him.[1]

The question highlighted by this modern parable is, is there anything between the collapse of a moderate and rational liberal faith which marked the Church at the beginning of the twentieth century and the drop-out sectarianism of the New Age or Fundamentalist sects at its end?

That is the driving question for the Church as it struggles with postmodernity. Can anything humanise our culture and is there anything to fill the vacuum of faith today?

A postmodern world

'Times they are a-changing!' and we are living in the midst of them. This can be very disturbing and can encourage us to be defensive and backward-looking because we are afraid. Or we can recognise that making sense of our life and seeking to humanise the emerging shape of our culture is the risky but essential journey for all who believe and trust in God.

The sort of change that is happening to us falls very broadly under the ugly term 'postmodernism'. It is not the purpose of this book to enter into a detailed analysis of postmodern philosophy. It is its purpose to recognise that, ugly though the term is, it does represent truth about the state of our culture. We do live in an emerging postmodern world. That is nothing to be afraid of. Indeed, seen in the right setting of spiritual understanding it offers opportunity for the flourishing of our life in community.

Postmodernism represents an acceptance of the diversity of our life today. It is deeply sceptical of all universals and especially of imposed ones. It holds to the idea that we construct the framework of ideas within which we live and these constructs are multiple. They cannot claim a universal demand upon any of us. They are self-chosen.

That poses a special challenge – either we discover a way of living together in peaceful and mutually understanding community or we all retreat into our distinctive self-ordered ghettos and watch our culture disintegrate. If we accept that the strength of postmodernism is in its rejections of the failures of modernism rather than in some dogmatic assertion of the lack of coherence in our common life, then it may open doors to a different and hopeful future. That is where the engagement of those whose journey involves a search for an experience of God might yet hold something of profound value for our culture. That is the journey to be explored in this book.

The task in front of us

The establishment and maintenance of a peaceful and ordered society requires great vision and wisdom. So much of human history is evidence of the contrary. Sectarianism, nationalism and unbridled individualism have led communities into varying levels of conflict and violence. We humans find it very hard to live together in peace and order. The creation of societies within which individuals and local communities are able to pursue their several vocations without hindrance is an extremely difficult business.

This is especially so in societies which are themselves a mixture of different cultures and beliefs and classes. Many are the places in our world where divisions of belief and political will have created intractable problems for the continued peace of the community. The lethal combination of divided political aspirations and religious traditions in the north of Ireland is a sad reminder of this problem within our own United Kingdom. The struggles of Croats, Bosnians and Serbs in the former lands of Yugoslavia reflect old historic conflicts between Catholics, Orthodox and Islamic societies. In the Middle East the complex agendas and contrasting aspirations of Jews and Arabs, Christian, Muslim and Jew, Sunni and Shiite, Armenian and Orthodox leave us all bewildered by the kaleidoscope of differing claims and histories.

The story is not new. Many of these struggles have their roots deep in history. Ancient disputes seem to reappear over and over again. The story of Christianity in Europe has been splattered with the blood of those who were considered to be heretical and a threat to good order by those who happened to carry power in the Church in their day and community. Throughout small groups of people of other faiths – most notably Jewish people – have suffered times of great and wicked abuse as power has been used to defend perceived orthodoxies.

We ought not to be surprised, therefore, that modern democratic societies have tried to solve the problem of pluralism and of peace by a principle of tolerance leaving people to follow their own beliefs and values. Both religion and morality have been left to the sphere of private conscience. Only if there is proven harm to the individual would society intervene. So it is assumed that plural cultures need to be secular rather than religious if they are to be held together.

These ideas have been upheld by frameworks of law and human rights provision which try to protect the interests and humanity of all members whatever their race, gender or belief. These developments have added much to the decency of society and are vital to its future health. When we say these changes are to be welcomed 'in principle' we open up a debate which we are often reluctant to enter. What principles and values undergird such provision? If we are afraid of too strong a moral and belief basis for society, from what resources are we to draw the values which will help us all to hold faith with the common decencies of a good society?

We live with a dilemma. Our experience makes us fearful of universal solutions which threaten imposition on unwilling minorities – so the postmodern love of diversity and distaste for all universals is attractive. On the other hand we long for a sense of community and know that we need some basis for mutual understanding if we are to live together in peace and freedom.

It is that great difficulty we have in sustaining such a decent and human society which leads us to consider the need for deeply held beliefs and values as vital to the health of a pluralist society. It is possible that secularism, unwittingly, is the enemy rather than the friend of civilised social order. A plural society may well need strong values and roots deeply embedded in ethical and, for believers, spiritual principles which will help it resist the age-old tendencies in human behaviour towards division, conflict and destruction. If we are to resist the powerful forces at work within us and within our communities towards such evil ends, then each person and each community will need a well-developed social conscience. Conscience leads us to values and beliefs.

This possibility needs exploring. Maybe Christian vision might yet help humanise and unite a truly postmodern world enabling all to live in freedom enjoying and benefiting from the changing patterns of a multi-cultural community.

We are sometimes cut off from this line of argument by the notion that since religion – and the Church in particular – has done so much damage in our history we should reject any idea that spiritual life and truth have anything to contribute.

If for one moment we accepted that line of argument it would be tantamount to accepting that the gospel, which alone gives sense and meaning to Christianity and to the Church, has nothing to offer in the struggle for a more human and stable world.

The failures and wickednesses of the Church must not be allowed to confuse the issue. An honest acceptance of the moral and spiritual failure of the Church to help protect freedom and justice cannot be escaped. We will be looking at the way the Church's witness has been emasculated by its prophetic failures in our own century. These are matters for deep penitence and an honest acceptance of responsibilities for the evils we have perpetrated. They are not, however, a reason for us to abandon the field of argument concerning the basis for a good society.

Indeed, it is difficult to see how the Church could have survived for so long with such loyalty from so many of every walk of life if its impact on human life has been so universally bad. Like any other institution made up of human beings the Church has a mixed history. The question concerns the validity of what it believes – not its manifest culpability in failing to be loyal to its faith. It is the vision to which the Church points people, rather than the institution itself, which is the truth and power which has captured so many in human history. All human institutions fail but the convictions which brought them into being are more durable than the forms in which they arrived.

If the Church is a fragile and weak instrument through

which people have caught a vision of something better for all, it should not surprise us that it is often tempted to reduce the vision of God to manageable proportions. We keep that vision within the Church or worse still we suggest that the Church is the vision rather than the vehicle. Along that road of religious reductionism lies the mistaken view that the transforming power of the Kingdom of God is something only Christians benefit from. That can even lead on to the suggestion that those who are not Christians are the enemy of the Kingdom and wholly excluded from the beauty of the gospel hope. The Church becomes arrogant, defensive and introspective. Other faiths and cultures become threats. So the vision fades and the glimpse of something better for all creation fades away into the darkness of a culture caught in conflict and decline.

We will have to think afresh about the meaning of our faith in God and how such faith connects or fails to connect with human endeavour today. At the heart of the cultural debate, as we need to have it in the Christian community, is the doctrine of God. That is because the essential issue is, can we believe in God and if faith is possible, what is its meaning?

One of the reasons for looking again at the possibility that religious beliefs and experience may have vital things to contribute to the perpetual task of seeking peace and goodness in society is Christianity's persistence. It has shown remarkable powers of resilient life. Its emergence from the shadows of Stalinism in Eastern Europe is a contemporary example. People kept the memory of faith alive in the most appalling conditions at different moments in the twentieth century. The challenge now is to see whether this re-emerging Church can help societies in transition to make the change and find a new age of human flourishing. Battered by the oppression of secular atheistic Stalinism and confused by the collusions it was sometimes drawn into with the Soviet state, the Church and the faith survived. It survived as much in the memory of the people as it did in its own order.

It is clear that this has, to a degree, happened in the past.

Art is often a measure of the state of culture. It is witness to the life of a community. Even in the heart of the repression of the 1920s and 30s in Russia writers and musicians continued their work and spoke through art of a different vision and hope. Art, even when it has no overt faith, can be the other side of the same reality as religion in these circumstances – an expression of the deepest longings of the human spirit. Like religion it can collude with the corruption of power and the debasement of human life. It becomes a tool of oppression. For example, in the sphere of music witness the music at Hitler's rallies, in the world of sculpture see the dominant statues of the people's leaders in the Maoist regime in China, or in the realm of the abuse of drama and the stage consider the banal dramas of the Revolution put out in the days of the height of Soviet power. Yet, art like religion, because of its exploration of reality and truth, is always a threat to those who shut the world up into a structure of ideas and power designed to keep things as they are.

Religious themes have touched deep parts of the soul of different communities and individuals and this has found expression in the art of each generation. Human creativity has been captivated by the story of the gospel whether it is the magical biblical drawings of Rembrandt or the great churches of Medieval Europe or the development of learning and scholarship. As we stand in front of the great icons of Orthodoxy or hear again the mystery of T.S. Eliot's poetry are we not often drawn into the mystery of which they speak? We too find the wellsprings of our own being touched and envigorated.

In comparison with these things how barbarous and grey appears the worlds of Marxist Leninist societies in the twentieth century. How destructive are those who tore down the orders of faith. Consider the human and cultural havoc of the Maoists and their successors who seek to crush the heritage of the people of Tibet! Religious and secular iconoclasm – a persistent streak of philistine puritanism – seems to be closely allied to a denial of freedom and a need to impose an ideological order even on unwilling peoples. Yet all history tells us that if faith offers to its adherents something vital to their humanity no amount of oppression can destroy its seeds of hope. Artists and communities of faith may yet keep alive a vision of something better. The day surely comes when the climate changes and things long since considered dead come to life again!

The twentieth century has been a brutal one. Hitler and Stalin represent the crude and gross endeavours at secularising our humanity and making it serve their deluded and restricted purposes. That has been mirrored in the East in the appalling experience of Mao's cultural revolution and the aftermath of the abuses of state power in China. Tiannamen Square is symbolic of the failure of Maoism to deliver what once was promised.

Western democracies have experienced different forms of the power of secularism. These forces have had a subtle and damaging effect upon religious faith. In democratic societies people are free to pursue their religion without hindrance. That is a welcome feature of any civilised society. Yet, in our setting, this has led to the assumption that religion is a private matter belonging to the domestic sphere of life. It has little or no relevance to our social and political life. The crude version of this is seen on those occasions when politicians tell Church leaders to stick to their own business – saving souls rather than seeking to influence the character of public life. Yet, given our history, this is quite extraordinary. We belong to a civilisation whose roots go deep into Christian belief.

The Church has had a major part in shaping our history. In some European societies, including our own, this is still recognised in the relationship formed between Church and state. That constitutional position expresses a historic recognition that the Church has a pivotal role in guarding the spiritual and moral foundations of our culture. This has created temptations for the Church about the importance of power and position. The Church has sometimes slipped into the tempting but false role of forming itself as an alternative

source of power in the public sphere. Medieval popes sometimes fell into that trap. In the midst of the changes taking
place in our own society the way the Church relates to the
social order will have to be restructured. The old order of
the establishment has no future to it. Yet the reformation
of the Church will need to rescue it from the privatised
position it holds in the Western world. Both the privileges of
power and the marginalisation of congregationalism will have
to be resisted. It is from within the Churches' own rationale
and spiritual life that it will need to find the resources for
fulfilling its task within the corporate life of a community.
What the Church needs to challenge is the assumption, so
prevalent in democratic societies, that our corporate life can
be carried forward without articulating the basic beliefs and
values which have the power to humanise us all.

The danger of a society which acknowledges only a minimal
basis for its common life is that it can become a competing
ground for conflicting values and aspirations with few
resources for resolving conflict. Its cohesion is fragile. Indeed,
its unity may depend on factors which themselves offer few
guarantees of its continuity. If, for example, democracies are
dependent on maintaining and even increasing standards of
material prosperity, their future cannot be guaranteed.
Democracy surely needs a more substantial basis than that.
An evolutionary optimism which looks for a steady progress
towards unending material prosperity is dependent upon the
notion that we are in full control of our destiny. One of
the reasons there is so much disenchantment with the modernism of the twentieth century is its failure to deliver. Whilst
the abandonment of a desire for shared convictions and values
may be the least desirable aspect of the postmodern culture
its rejection of the unsuccessful uniformity of progressive
modernism strikes many chords with reality.

Yet we may well wonder, in the twentieth century, whether
in fact our democratic procedures in Western societies have
a stronger foundation. There has been so much emphasis
upon the technical matters of getting the economy right and

on things concerning wealth creation and our standard of living that we may well ask what would happen if we passed through a prolonged period of economic and material diffi- culty? Twice in our own century the unity of our society has been recovered by the reality of war. It is a strange thing to hear those who remember war in Britain talking positively about its impact upon the cohesion of our communal sense of purpose. Is war the only way we can achieve this?

The present re-emergence in Europe of powerful nationalist and even fascist forces are a dark reminder of the abyss at the end of periods of economic hardship. It may be highly dangerous to make material prosperity the basis for managing our diversity. The crumbling of such a fragile foun- dation can only lead to the various sectors of our pluralist community returning to tribal securities and thence to conflict and so to battle. It is a frightening scenario. Returning to the forest is the stuff of romantic dreams. It has no place in the sophisticated world of modern communication and choice.

The vision of a common cultural and spiritual base for society, within which the diversity of the many is not only tolerated but valued, needs exploring afresh. It will require both the Church and the several leaders of society to purge themselves of all imperialisms and their beguiling sins. The vision of God offered to the world in Jesus Christ not only supports but requires us to pursue excellence and beauty in our common life and in the development of our community.

The gospel story for our time

What are we offered? Nothing less than the mystery of God in whose being are beauty and love more attractive than our deepest imaginings. In the gospel stories we are presented with the experience of people who, in encountering Jesus, experienced God in richer and newer ways. This experience was not a destruction and denial of their past but a transform- ation of it. In the story in John 4 of the encounter between Jesus and the woman at the well we see horizons being widened, sectarianism challenged and an experience of God which is inclusive. The argument about where God was to be properly worshipped – on this mountain or that – was transcended by the encounter with Jesus.[2] Here is divine love which neither destroys us nor allows us to stay where we are.

The Gospels present Jesus as someone who conducted his ministry in ways which require new vision and a moving forward in more inclusive and less sectarian ways. He is above the battle between Pharisee and Sadducee, accepting and proclaiming the resurrection contra Sadducee and refusing the petty bourgeois legalism of Pharisee.[3] His teaching transcends the division of Jew and Samaritan. His parables reversed the public perceptions which were divisive. The story we call the Good Samaritan is a striking and permanent testimony to this side of Jesus' ministry.[4] In similar ways his behaviour and teaching subtly but powerfully transcend the divisions of the sexes – he affirmed Mary as she joined with everyone else in sitting at his feet instead of retiring to the kitchen to prepare the meal. It is Martha who needed liberating. Mary had discovered a better way. These stories could be multiplied.[5]

The struggle of Christianity has always been about inclusiveness. The Church has found it very hard to be Christian. It has frequently collapsed into repressive cultures requiring conformity rather than enabling liberty. The vision of God in the faith of Christ is essentially and eternally inclusive. Sectarianism and partisanship cannot be squared with the testimony of Jesus. Every time we take that restrictive path we find the face of God staring at us in Christ from the lives of those we exclude. In the twentieth century the face of Christ has looked at us from the faces of the enemy far too often. We have to find the secret of inclusive ways of being and of living.

Thus a society which seeks to root its history and culture in this religious tradition is called not just to tolerate communities of other faiths or of none – but positively to protect or enable them. The gospel story encourages a deep respect for the humanity and liberty of others. The challenge which each makes of the other concerning the nature of reality, the meaning of truth and the direction of human affairs is not allowed to destroy the common bonds of the life we share within the meaning of the love of God. Jesus travelled across cultural barriers and made the challenge to all without exception of the life of the Kingdom of God.

This leads us to something Christians have had to learn to value – liberty of conscience. There have been times when the Church has been tempted to force or manipulate the consciences of individuals and undermine the cultural integrity of communities. The bond of love between God's being and our being rests essentially on a sense of the bond being entered into with freedom. Enforced faith, in other words, is destructive of faith. Freedom and faith, respect for conscience and love of God are indestructibly held together. We have to recognise the debt owed by our culture to the Enlightenment which led the way towards a recognition of the sacredness of conscience. The Enlightenment, we need to remember, came after a century or more of religious war, conflict and destruction. Truth meets us from many directions.[6]

This marks one of the closest points for the relationship of religious belief as understood by Christians and the principles of democracy. The inclusive love of God is active through a process of freedom and risk. The religious foundations of a free society and of a flourishing plural community life are always enabling ones. When Christians, therefore, enable their brothers and sisters of other traditions to practise their beliefs in line with the dictates of their own conscience they are bearing testimony to something close to the heart of God. There have been delightful and symbolically important moments when Christians have helped other faith communities establish themselves.[7] The discussion about allowing other faith communities to use buildings which were made for Christian worship should be understood in this setting of conviction. We must not deny the truth as it has been revealed in Jesus.

When seen in this context, democracy is not a system whereby one group or party gains supremacy over others. It is rather a philosophy of society designed to ensure that all participate and accept a common responsibility for the health of the whole community. The outcome is that all covenant to live in peace and mutual respect. Politically, democracy is about how all find representation in systems of government. This is parallel to the idea of liberty of conscience. These values may be established and sustained by our spiritual inheritance. The structure of beliefs and the consequent values which have helped form our culture have deep power within them for the benefit of democratic communities. To sacrifice this for the grey monotony and fragility of a society, rooted in secular materialism is something that ought to alarm all people of good will and imagination. As we shall see there may be surprises for us as we consider who is furthering this journey of the spirit today for the future?

There are many other outcomes for a plural society when it has the courage to see itself in a wide context of beliefs and values. One of them, which is more important than sometimes we think, is the capacity for such a society to become a creative and imaginative community. The state of the arts is often a sign of the health of society. The tortured expressions of artistic life in the twentieth century are testimony to a tortured and violent history. Perhaps there is no other community in which the struggle for a humanity rooted in a sense of deeper realities which lead us to goodness and hope is experienced than the community of art. It is not without significance that one of the most creative political thinkers of our age – Vaclav Havel, President of the Czech Republic – is someone whose life has been shaped by the agony of Eastern Europe and by his own artistic imagination. Maybe the poets, the painters, the musicians, the architects and the sculptors can help us not only understand where we are but help us recover vision for where we might go. It is

Havel who constantly reminds us that Europe faces a moment of choice and that if it is to make it a moment of hope it must recover its spiritual and moral integrity.[8]

The Church, weakened and battered as it is by secularism, can contribute to the future by its sympathetic collaboration with the world of the arts. Again, imperialist patronage has to give way to sensitive recognition of the vital contribution made by all whose skill and insight open windows into the human soul, the nature of our culture and even into divine reality.

Great art is never sectarian. It is always opening doors rather than closing them. It is part of the lifeblood of an open society. It keeps things alive which might otherwise so easily die.

For too long we have allowed a minimalist concept of common values to be the key to success in managing a plural society. Reductionism is a killer of much that is good. It brings us below the best and dims the vision of the future. It is pragmatic and orientated to the present. We need a wider and deeper vision if the deterioration of our culture and our common life is not to collapse into an age of recrimination, conflict and destruction. We must explore whether the resources of faith have a word for this task. A postmodern world has nothing to fear from such an exploration. The affirmation of the essential freedom which belongs to our humanity at the heart of its being goes hand in hand with the search for those values and visions which hold our life together and help us keep the flame of freedom alive.

Section I

Understanding God in a Postmodern Age

Conversation which opens up the possibility of God for people today seems so difficult for us. We would rather talk about church or aspects of action in the world.

Yet the essential issue facing us in a postmodern setting concerns the structure of reality. May we – dare we – think in terms of the divine life and being in the face of what we know and how we see the world today? That has become a crisis issue for a culture reticent of any imposed universals. If religious faith and experience require an abandonment of the freedom and possibility of our culture they will be seen as repressive. There have been enough times in the history of the Church where faith has become a way of enforced conformity and so of repression.

The hope that religious experience – the sense of the being and even of the love of God – might help us find a way of shared life which does not compromise the diverse and unpredictable nature both of the cosmos and of human life within it is the one we need to explore.

Is the world open to love and to the hope of freedom or is it just a meaningless bundle of unrelated constructs of the human mind? Can we come together without destroying one another or are we left to the life of the jungle? Postmodernism will not let us off the hook by allowing an easy route back into universals and imposed absolutes. That drives us to the mystery of all being. When we arrive at that question are we faced with nothingness and a silence that is void? Or is there a pulsating life and a energy of love filling the silence of the world we inhabit today?

1

The Silence of God

The death of God was pronounced by Nietzsche[1] long before we experienced the appalling wickedness of Auschwitz. Auschwitz raises the critical questions of belief implicit in Nietzsche's work. The Holocaust is the point of reference for all serious theology post 1945. Talk about God, if that is possible for people today, must happen in the face of this reality. J.B. Metz speaks of this being the determinant of all German theology.[2] We must say that it is to be critical for all theology done in a Western context. If we cannot look at Auschwitz and speak of God we must give up the endeavour.

The matter may be more far-reaching than that. Nietzsche spoke not only of the death of God but of the death of humanity. The dreadful abuses of the Nazi tyranny, meted out to the Jews in particular, open the door to the terrifying possibility that we have not only lost God but we have lost our humanity as well. It is not surprising to find the postmodernist voices rejecting all universals and encouraging us to break up the uniformity and allow humankind to retreat into a multitude of separate and distinct worlds of its own construction. Look what the twin pillars of European civilisation – Christianity and the Enlightenment – produced in our own time. In the middle of the great century of scientific and social progress, in the midst of the remorseless march of history towards a new future of equality and freedom, and in the heart of Christian civilisation, an act of unspeakable evil was perpetrated among us and we let it happen. Does that not throw into question both the inheritance of the Church and of humanism? The postmodernist mood fits the need of the end

5

of such a century as this. Neither God nor humanity can be trusted again.

We have been especially troubled by our inability to explain what has happened. Words, ideas, notions of history seem to fall well short of the sheer power of these events to destroy what we thought we had so successfully created. People who visit the Yad Voshem memorial in Jerusalem are reduced to silence. Standing at the places which bring to the memory of our civilisation the pain of the past, words retreat. There must be silence. Even tears seem to be trite. The memorial, the record of our inhumanity, the sheer scale of what a line of huts and a few gas chambers represent, has to be word enough. In the silence is the unbroken scream of the disaster of our civilisation. Six million voices silenced in this way cry out in our silence.

There is a special particularity in these matters. This is for us to face. We have to accept the contextualisation of these matters, even if their import has affected the life of the whole of humanity. It was in Europe, in the twentieth century, in a nation still suffering the guilt of one terrible war and which was not greatly helped by its neighbours nor by the failure of capitalism following that war, that these things happened. So it is those who are heirs to the Christian/Enlightenment culture of Europe who must respond and see if there is any way to move on.

The question of silence in the face of evil draws us to the question of the nature of the universe and of the meaning of our life within it. Is the silence one of the death of God and even of humanity? Much of course did die. It was not only the millions of people consigned to the gas chambers. Christendom died and with it notions of the competence of the Church to be the guardian of our culture. The notion of the steady march of progress died and with it concepts of the movement of history towards an ideologically pure end. Not everyone has come to terms with these bereavements. Both Christendom and notions of progress have still to be buried. Without doubt they are dead. But their corpses still attract followers. Neither a benign Christianised culture nor the Marxist struggle had the power to hold back the dread forces which let such destruction and brutality loose in our midst. The confident assertions of the twentieth century of having arrived – of having found the answers to our social or personal histories – are shattered by the sheer scale of the evil we have encountered.

First responses

There have been a mixture of responses.

Twentieth-century Liberalism

The liberal response has been cautious of all ideology and lays stress on the liberties and rights of all individuals. The values we need are only those essential for a free and peaceful community. The state, and all forms of corporate power, need to stay well clear of all ideologies. It is the individual who should be in the driving seat – society is secondary to the individual. People should be free to pursue their own beliefs but there should be no collective commitment to one as opposed to another. The secular state and democratic institutions are the protection individuals need from any return to the nightmares of the past. The politics and culture of this liberal world range from moderate democratic socialism to liberal free market conservatism. The way to keep the 'isms', which had caused such damage in Europe in the 30s and 40s and continued to do so in the East until the collapse of Soviet Leninist domination, at bay is to play them down. A stress on the rights of the individual, pragmatic political life, the containment of pluralism by the depoliticising of religion and the careful control of the educational system lest it become ideologically bound, are all ways of keeping a secular, free society open and peaceful.[3]

Much post 1945 politics has looked like this across the Western world. Even the establishment of the State of Israel was based on a secular and mildly democratic form of socialism. Earlier in the century, in response to the collapse of the old Turkish order, after 1918, Ataturk established an openly secular state for the Islamic people of modern Turkey. The founder of modern Turkey wanted to play down any idea of an ideological commitment by the modern Turkish State. Modernity went hand in hand with secularisation.

Theology reformed

In the field of theological thought another response was to lay stress on the utter distinctiveness of the Divine Word in Jesus Christ. Christianity is a revealed religion rooted in God's own free and unfettered act. It is not a branch of philosophy, or a political creed or a spiritual prop for secular living. It is the gift of God's own self to the world in Christ, free, life-giving and creative of a new order. This powerful Word made known to the world in Jesus Christ passes judgement on the world, and offers salvation and the fulfilment of the mystery of the divine purpose of love. Over and against the blasphemies of the twentieth century stands the gospel Word calling the Church to resist the idolatrous claims of the corruption of power and the arrogant assertion of human achievement as the secret of the meaning of our lives. Karl Barth was the great twentieth-century exponent of this theology.[4]

The Barthian revolution in theology has played a powerful role in stiffening the faith of the Church in the face of the abusive menaces of twentieth-century corporate life. Its emphasis upon the uniqueness of the Word of God has enabled it to resist any dependency upon the visible Church as the source of hope for humanity. Only God, as revealed in Jesus Christ, can offer hope. Confidence in God, existential commitment to the wonder and saving effect of the Word made flesh, rescues us from having to find confidence either in Christendom or in the reasoned endeavours of our struggle towards an enlightened humanity. The absolute is in God and nowhere else. This conviction acts as a line of judgement against all absolutising tendencies in human living. All is relative to the Word.

This neo-orthodoxy at the heart of the twentieth century had many faces. In British theology it is to be found in the work of P.T. Forsyth,[5] who like Barth after him, saw the nakedness of late nineteenth-century liberal progressive theologies to cope with the demands of the modern and corporate world. Only a strong sense of the integrity of revealed theology – rooted in faith in the gracious action of God upon the world – had the guts to meet the challenge of the twentieth century.

In America, in a different setting Reinhold Niebuhr got hold of the issue of power in corporate life and of the inability of the optimistic philosophies and theologies of the early twentieth century to meet up to its realities.[6] An optimistic liberalism stressing individual compassion seemed powerless in the face of the corporate power of General Motors in Detroit in the recessionary years of the twenties and thirties. Only a theology which could cope with the demands of power and of justice would speak to the contemporary human condition. Niebuhr's work influenced a generation of politicians on both sides of the Atlantic, many of whom had had to work out their political creeds in the face of the corporate evils of the mid-twentieth century.

Hope for liberation

If Barthianism did something about cleansing the mind of the Church of its dependency upon its cultural inheritance whether expressed ecclesiologically or theologically, liberation movements endeavoured to cleanse the Enlightenment inheritance in like fashion. The gentle bourgeois evolution, through science and politics, towards a liberal and civilised society, had to give way to the struggle to overturn the bastions of power threatening the humanity of the marginalised.

If there were to be no more gas chambers then there must be struggle for freedom for the oppressed.

In the postwar period liberation movements were fed by the persistence of oppression both political and economic. In its paranoid obsession with defeating Marxism the USA sustained and supported a number of brutal and repressive regimes across the world. Progressive liberal politics seemed to have no energy to do anything for the massed poor of the world exploited by both international capitalism and local political dictatorships. Grassroots liberation movements grew and were fed on a diet of optimistic modern Marxism.

Both at a level of thought and of action these movements have brought together Marxists and Christians.[7] The way to bear witness to the hope of a better future for those threatened with exclusion is by sharing in the historic struggle for freedom. From a theological perspective it is the sense of incarnation – the taking part in the action of history in the particular – which is the driving power of Christian presence. It is at the heart of the meaning of liberation theology as it both calls for commitment to the praxis of history and for the formation of the new community as foretaste of what is to be the hope for all.[8] The classroom for modern theology is with the poor in their struggle for freedom and for justice in community.

There are many faces to modern liberation struggles. They may be predominantly political – as in the struggle for liberation in Zimbabwe or South Africa – or more cultural in their politics as in the feminist struggle for freedom from a male-dominated culture and social order. Within all these movements are massive debates about the shape of thinking and practice to be pursued. The debate about violence and non-violence, about the efficacy of the Marxist as opposed to the postmodernist analysis of power, about when and whether to participate in the system which it is struggling to replace. Neither liberation movements nor liberation theology are monochrome. They are at one in opting for direct confrontation with the prevailing power in the culture to effect change. They do not believe that the liberal way of evolution works for the marginalised. Direct action alone will shift the balance of power.

The outcomes sought are to do with freedom from oppression – however that is defined – and justice in the assertion of the equal power of all, so there is a demand for a power shift towards those believed to have been excluded. That can only be achieved if those who are powerless take responsibility for their own liberation and act in the historical and cultural context of oppression in which they find themselves.

Liberation theologies have been aimed at allying the message of Jesus with the hopes and aspirations of the marginalised and a call upon the Church to stand at one with the struggle of the victims. That challenge to the Church involves the Church accepting that it has colluded with the oppressive characteristics of power and that it must be reformed from within by a process of theological renewal – the doing of theology and the reforming of the Church in the midst of the struggles of the excluded.

These three ways of responding to the issues raised for our culture by the devastating experiences of the abuses of power and of innocent peoples in the twentieth century all have achievements to record.

The liberal character of secular democratic societies post 1945 has been one of peace and order balanced with a measure of freedom and justice. Whole generations of people are, as a result, suspicious of ideological approaches to community life.

The Barthian insistence on the freedom of God as expressed in the Word made flesh in Jesus Christ has acted as a constant reminder to the Church that it needs critical distance as well as human solidarity with the cultures within which it forms its life. There is a provisionality about all human achievement including the achievement of the Church when it is confronted with the meaning of the gospel Word which is offered to us by the mystery of God's free act. The sharp edge between the Kingdom of God and the kingdoms of this world is the defence against all who would confuse the creator with the created order.

The struggle for freedom, which has been the persistent lot of so many in the latter half of the twentieth century, has brought a sense of hope and dignity to multitudes of those who would otherwise be forgotten in the predominant and unchallenged power of the prevailing culture. We are all still learning to change our ways of seeing the world and its people so that the oppressive forces at work in all culture can be both contained and radically transformed. Many of these stories are still being told by those caught up in their daily realities.

Yet all three contemporary responses leave us with questions and an open door to face a different future. Liberal politics finds pluralism difficult to manage and is constantly tempted to seek for universal and easy solutions and so fails to satisfy the need for community today. Its reticence about values fails to connect with the need for vision and direction in our common life. The radical 'no' of Barth to all forms of liberal humanistic theology runs the risk of leaving God on the sidelines of our living. Theology is left in a world of its own and you either believe it or you don't. The connection between the eternal and the temporal cannot just be dismissed and avoided. Liberation struggles, however justified their cause, lead their followers into the temptation to abuse power in the interest of the justified end. They fail to find sufficient critical distance from the culture of liberation itself and from its failures. The overriding demand of the good end – setting people free – can be compromised by a casualness about the means – what can be justified when you think you are in a war. The classic immediate example of this danger is in the growing evidence of the abuses perpetrated by the ANC in their African strongholds outside South Africa on some of their suspects. These things happened during the years of the struggle. War backed up by a legitimate sense of the validity of the cause can be dangerous.

The postmodern world has grown suspicious that the full challenge of our century has not been met by these responses. So we face a new century looking again at the adequacy of politics and faith and at the meaning of our humanity when confronted with the challenge of liberation.

Learning from the silence

The silence of Auschwitz leaves us with a crucial question. Is the silence empty or not? That is the dilemma of postmodernism. Is this a way of seeing which necessarily must resist all endeavours to fill the silence or to find something positive and creative in it? Or is it simply a caution – a necessary protest – against all universalising forces which refuse to face the joyful and creative reality of our diversity and plurality? Nietzsche thought the silence was empty.[9] Our dependence on any meaning given to us by faith in some universal and omnipotent deity had to be abandoned. We had to learn to live in the awful freedom from such comforting protection. For Nietzsche issues which theologians and philosophers believed to be questions of truth are matters of interpretation – even manipulative interpretation – and of power. It is the power of religion, both in its corporate identity in the structures of priesthood and authority in the Church and in the dependencies it creates in individuals, which is so destructive of humanity. Words and language are used to hold people subject. Filling the silence is dangerous because of the way language can be used as a tool of knowledge and of power. God is dead and the silence is indeed empty. Religion is a construct of power.

Auschwitz has sharpened the question. If God is dead then we must face the distinct possibility that humanity is dead as well. Far from this liberation from religion being a moment of freedom and possibility it becomes a moment when the world realises that the silence is indeed empty and that we are alone. If alone, who and what will protect us from ourselves and from the abuses of power which Nietzsche so fully expounds? Is our life a struggle in relation to issues of power? If so, what comfort is that to the victims and the survivors of Auschwitz?

The alternative road is to recognise the importance of the dismantling of the structures of thought, religion and politics which failed to hold back the lethal forces of the Nazi terror and all events of its kind in our century, and then to explore the meaning of the consequent silence to see if there are some signals of things which can help us hold both our sanity and our humanity. It is possible the silence is not vacant.

What sort of silence are we encountering in this post-modern world? There is the silence of not knowing – a reticence about our capacity to understand. That is by no means an empty silence. It is full of possibility. A culture which knows its limits might learn and grow. Limits are what we have to understand as we turn from one century to another. The twentieth century has seen the end of the road of our self-proclaimed omniscience. Because we know so much more we know so much less. We know what fanaticism fed by insecurity can do and we have seen the utter weakness and helplessness of people of good will in the face of such forces. We know what people can do and we have no credible explanation. We wonder at the great advances of genetic science and of quantum mechanics. We are fascinated by the insights of the human sciences into our behaviour. We are confused and driven to distraction by the depths of awfulness into which people are drawn. The devastation of the world and its peoples leave us groping for some wisdom. We have no words because we have to travel on down the road of self-knowledge and the meaning of our life.

Such silence calls not for a fatalistic abandonment of the search for truth and humanity but for much more listening. It may seem strange to speak of listening to the silence. Our words, our knowing, our endeavours have produced a great deal of noise and even more trouble. A patient listening is inescapable if we are to find a way forward.

Silence can be a mixture of shock and awe. We look at

what has happened and we are shocked. There is nothing to say – no words which can capture for us the revelation of what has happened. We see what is going on and we are amazed – so mind-blown that again words fail. Either in the face of the depths of evil or the extraordinary wonders of the world we are looking into a reality which draws us towards another dimension of knowing and of truth. It is as if we are drawn towards hell or heaven – not as places like other places we can describe – but experiences which draw us into the silence of being.

That leads us on to the inner experience of silence – the protest of the spirit of the person against the abuses of tyranny wherever it is to be found. One of the things which tyranny searches out is the inner silence of the person – our own being. Is this silence empty? If it is, then tyranny is triumphant because it may have its way with humanity as it wills. Power is the only reality which makes sense. But every story of the assertion of the dignity of the person in the face of appalling abuse is a sign of hopefulness that the silence within is not empty. When Jews who survived Auschwitz were asked whether they could believe in God after such unspeakable experience there were those who said, we must not allow them to destroy our faith as they have destroyed our lives and families. That would be the final surrender. The strength of the inner silence of the few gave dignity to the multitudes who perished in such wretched brutality.

Then there is the silence of emptiness. Nothing is there. The biblical criticism of idols is not that they are not as effective as the God of Abraham, Isaac and Jacob. It is that they are no gods at all (Psalm 115:3–8). There is nothing there. The search for meaning and truth will falter if it is presented in terms of *something* being there. Gods who fill gaps, or are bigger versions of the most powerful things we know, or are present as a measurable force are no gods. They are not there. The mystics who speak of God as nothing are making the point that God cannot be something. If we are drawn into the silence of our condition to discover, we are faced with the other beyond us – the mystery that makes possible growth and journeying in truth both inwardly in the person and outwardly in the culture.

The beginnings of faith are possible in the broken and scattered culture of a postmodern world when we turn from the idols of the gods who are something and who are discovered to be nothing. With the postmodern world we can resist the universals we have made by our reason or our religion. The bringing together of the broken pieces of our lives must rest in a deeper communion.

It is to that possibility that Jesus bears witness. He spoke with authority – not as the Scribes and Pharisees. He broke through the ritual divisions of the Palestinian world drawing a Samaritan woman beyond the religion of Samaria or even of Jerusalem. He said not a word in the face of gross injustice and violent abuse of his own person – a silence which amazed Pilate (Matthew 27:11–14). He went alone into the desert and the hills to commune with a Father beyond all fathers and resisted thereby the Near Eastern idolatry of the family. He had a Father and a family beyond the natural family.

Those who encountered these things knew themselves to be in the presence not of the wooden gods of tradition but of a living and eternal God in whom all people and all reality take shape and learn the way of freedom. The silence was full and alive and among them. Their own being found new depths as a result in forgiveness, in love and in the discovery of new truth.

If we cannot return to a form of universal culture – even an enlightened Christian one – there is no future in simple disintegration. Everyone doing what is right in their own eyes may rescue us in the immediate from an imposed tyranny but runs the risk of the sort of chaos that leads into a new dark age and so to a different experience of tyranny. Romantic desires to rediscover the pagan myths which exercised so much power in the past or to return to some basic natural order of living lead us into darkness. This is another form of slavery – a bondage of the human spirit which is left to the fates because it has no structure of understanding which sustains the hope of freedom. There are aspects of the post-modernist culture which seem to want to take us further into the past – back to the forests!

What none of us can do is to deny the history we have been through. The task must surely, therefore, be one of moving on. The challenge is to find the roots of a decent and sustainable humanity in a sustainable history and a sustain-able environment. That requires us to perceive the possibilities of the postmodern. Into that we must take the constructive contributions of our time. The ideological caution of liberal secular democracy, whatever its limits, is a gain. The insistence on the priority of the dispossessed in the struggle for freedom is gain. And, in theological terms, the sense of awe and wonder in the face of the Other brings proportion and boundary to the exercise of power.

The task is to build. The destroying has run for long enough. It is in the open and multi-faced possibilities of our diverse and changing world that we might find confidence in the sense of being and wonder which draw us together in a shared and mixed journey of personal and social exploration. It was something of this confidence and freedom which people gained from being with Jesus. The silence, the pain, the empti-ness of their living became full of living hope in the encounter with his person, teaching and activity. The sense of promise which ran through their faith as rooted in their culture found fulfilment in this experience. The love which endures, the forgiveness which sets free, the life which is stronger than the grave, the power of redemptive suffering to transform and overcome the forces of darkness which hold people so firmly in their grip: all of these were the experience of people in the presence of Jesus.

The liberating effect included a sense that the range and diversity of human experience was welcomed and transfig-ured. Religion might insist on conformity to the Law and Custom. Politics might insist on a universal acknowledgement of the power of Rome. No such universalising insistences

17

were received by the people when they met Jesus. Rather he gave freedom to people to deepen their own sense of responsibility for the way they developed their own life and culture. That is why the tax collectors and the excluded found Jesus so attractive. He ate at their table and brought a sense of liberty through forgiveness which gave them the space to choose afresh the way they wanted to live.

Out of that grew a new community which had to come to terms with its own diversity. The temptation is to solve the problem by new demands for conformity. The creation of new power structures to tell everyone how it might work would be one way of trying to solve the issue. The other was to experience change through the demands of the new relationships. Just as all had been drawn into community because they had sensed the address to them of the Divine Love which was beyond them and other than their immediate experience, so they had to learn to live in communion with the others who had shared the experience. Life grew from the bottom up. The sense of the absolute and even of the universal lay not within them and could not be created by them without serious risk of abuse. It was beyond – coming towards them with liberating power.

If the community formed in the love experienced in the person of Jesus Christ had to learn to resist closing itself into structures and ideas which excluded those who found themselves addressed and liberated by the Divine Love, in no sense was that a minimalist experience. It was a life and community transforming journey. Nothing lay beyond its touch. The words, ideas, thoughts, prayers, pastoral practice of this community had to keep humanity open to the journey. That means that theology, liturgy, pastoral engagement and proclamation would have a sense of paradox about them. The mystery and the sense of the wholly other must not be allowed to collapse into new forms of idolatry, however orthodox they might seem to be. Humanity needs preserving from having to conform to the constructions of the deployment of our cultural and social power.

The possibility of faith – of the significance of the meaning of our silence – is in its capacity to keep the hope of freedom and growth alive across the diversity of a changing and often confusing world. If it does not offer the hope of this it is not following in the way of Jesus.

2

God and the Meaning of Freedom

The problem of the meaning of human freedom has troubled theologians since the early days of the Church. St Paul speaks of humankind and of creation as subject to the bonds of servitude and longing for freedom (Romans 8:18–24). The question of the freedom of the will divided Christian thinkers at the time of the Reformation. Luther's thesis entitled 'The Bondage of the Will' was a counterblast to the Erasmian tradition of Christian humanism which delighted in the possibilities of human freedom.[1] Luther and Calvin, following in the footsteps of Augustine, saw freedom and liberation as gifts of grace which are rooted in the gospel.[2] These are not to be seen as aptitudes of human life. Humanity lost its freedom in the Garden of Eden. It is recovered only in the saving grace of Jesus Christ. So the issue of human freedom has been a point of contention in theology for many centuries.

There is a particular twentieth-century edge to this critical question. The political struggle against the many faces of colonialism and, indeed, sheer tyranny has been a grim story of our own time. The imposition of one person's story upon another has been the cause of immense suffering and damage to humankind. Some of it has been very crude and brutal. Whether it is the story of racism and apartheid in Africa – a story yet to be told in its grim fullness – or the hideous nightmare of Fascism and the Nazi tyranny across Europe in the 1930s and 40s, it is a story which has stirred people to defend their humanity and that of others in the struggle for freedom.

Freedom has been a twentieth-century cry in the face of tyranny. Even within relatively free societies communities

20

of people have felt that the integrity of their own humanity has been under the shadow of the power of other and controlling ways of describing the culture. Women, for example, have lived under male definitions of their nature, place and role. Predominant sexual cultures have at best marginalised and at worst criminalised those whose life experience is different. Gay and Lesbian people tell some grim stories of the oppression and repression of their humanity. Many of us, if we have the courage to search within our own life experience, know moments when others have tried to define our own life according to their values and beliefs. We have had to resist or else face the possibility of some loss of the integrity of our own being. So there have been and continue to be cultural movements for personal and community liberation.

People who live under tyranny dream of freedom and seek to keep alive another story of human life and meaning. They draw strength from sharing in communities of suffering and oppression. In some of these the promise of freedom in Jesus Christ and the struggle for freedom from human tyranny come together and feed each other. There can be no understanding of the meaning of liberation theology in the last part of the twentieth century unless this subtle but powerful bond between the divine and the human stories of freedom is recognised. Something of this dynamic of freedom is to be found in aspects of the history of Trade Unionism in the development of industrial working life.[3] Men who, for example, were condemned to cut slate by candlelight in the slate mines of North Wales formed Trade Unions in the mines. They belonged to non-conformist Christian communities and their Trade Unionism was practised in the midst of prayer and worship. The fellowship of suffering in the slate mines was expressed in a world of faith and politics which could not be separated. In a similar way black people in North America, living with the wickedness of slavery and the persistence of racism long after the legal ending of slavery, kept their human dignity and vision of freedom alive in the sharing of the story of Jesus.[4] No one who has shared in the worship of the townships in South Africa in the days of apartheid could miss the indestructible bond between the vision of faith and the struggle for freedom.

This is paradoxical because these experiences were often opposed and hindered by the forces at work in the Church as well as in the powers of the political and cultural orders of the day. We know a good deal of the story of the Church's collusion with the Nazi heresy and its attack upon those who understood the meaning of what was going on. We also know of the difficulty the white Christian community had in facing up to the challenge of both racism and apartheid in Southern Africa. It was not just the Afrikaner communities which struggled with the heresy of racism. Caught in the vortex of the struggle many yielded to the temptation to find some rationalisation for the continuance of the prevailing and evil order. German Christians who opposed Hitler and white Christians who struggled to undo apartheid sometimes paid a heavy price within their own communities for their religious and moral courage.[5] It was almost as if the liberating story of Jesus linking with the sense of hope for a different future for those living under false and oppressive stories happened in spite of religion rather than because of it.

Yet the moral courage of the few speaks of the powerful hope of freedom which inhabits the hearts of many who live in different forms of bondage. So the question of freedom is a sharp and urgent one for all serious Christian thought and action and it is one the Church cannot afford to ignore in the light of its twentieth-century confusions.

The story has moved on

At both extremes the idea of freedom as essential to understanding reality has been under challenge by the developments of twentieth-century thought. At the macro level, what we now know about the sheer scale and form of the universe has transformed our understanding of our place in creation and of the possibility of both divine and human freedom. At the micro level the enormous strides made in genetic theory have opened again questions about the limits on human freedom and the measure to which our lives are determined by their genetic shape. Stephen Hawking[6] on the one side and Richard Dawkins[7] on the other represent the double edge of this challenge and both raise crucial theological and cultural questions.

Christians have sometimes responded to these discoveries and challenges by seeking for theological meaning in the things not yet understood. So we vacate the field of interpreting knowledge in cosmology or genetics and look for the meaning of God in the mysteries as yet unveiled. This presents serious problems for faith. If God is to be found in the gaps in human knowledge about the character of the universe and the mystery of the human person the possibility of belief is available on a rapidly diminishing field. We know so much more. The assumption that the study of the origin and shape of the universe and the structure of the human person are secular disciplines, divorced from questions of faith, is deeply mistaken. Yet the Church has so often proceeded as if this were the case. We have responded to the agendas set by others rather than contributed to the task of interpreting the meaning of what is being explored. It is not surprising to find Stephen Hawking raising theological questions towards the end of his book which are of this order. Now that we know all this what do we need God for?[8] Questions of meaning, however, are pressed in upon all of us by the shape of modern science. We are all having to think again about how what we know influences our understanding of the shape and meaning of both the universe and our own human lives.

The idea that what we discover determines the outcome of our view must be resisted. We cannot throw humankind into the power of various academic disciplines and philosophies, however attractive. We have to assume responsibility ourselves for interpreting what is offered. The thing works the other way round. How we view the world shapes how we receive new evidence and ideas. The development of a shape

23

of meaning has to make sense of knowledge. The art of theological thinking is to resist both the fundamentalist temptation to bring faith and knowledge into conflict (as, for example, in the fundamentalist resistance to evolutionary theory) and the subjection of faith to knowledge. That was the mistake which led to the errors of reductionism and positivism. These might suggest, for example, that genetic discovery is determinative of understanding the meaning of the human person in the universe. Such a view not only threatens our freedom but also implies a philosophic imperialism for particular scientific disciplines. There is a powerful interplay between our culture, our self-understanding of who we are, our place in the universe and the discoveries we make on the journey of living. We make sense of the freedom in love for which we yearn when we have the courage to keep the human story open.

One of the things postmodernism has done is to bring to our attention the many constructs we put upon our life. Michael Foucault, for example, in his work on the history of madness has sought to demonstrate that, in the Classical Age, there was a fundamental shift in the cultural and intellectual understanding which affected the way people both saw and responded to madness. He focuses on the issue of confinement.[9] Gary Cutting describes Foucault's view and approach in this way:

> Foucault, however, is not interested in the event of confinement for its own sake, but in the attitudes toward and perceptions of madness connected with it – what he repeatedly refers to as 'the Classical experience of madness'. The event of confinement is the sudden manifestation of a long-developing 'social sensibility'. The goal of his history of madness is to describe exhaustively this experience or sensibility and to show how it provided the basis for the modern psychiatric conception of madness as mental illness.[10]

In a powerful way he links the practice of confinement of

24

the poor, the beggars, the unemployed and the mad with a growing bourgeois morality concerned with the family and rooted in both Enlightenment concepts of reason and a Calvinist work ethic. The construct we have put upon the experience shapes the way we respond to the evidence and form our culture and social order. So it is important to reflect on the way we perceive the world. There have been many criticisms of Foucault but few would doubt the importance of his thought and of our need to understand the importance of the constructions we place upon reality.

Another example of the way we have allowed the constructs of others to determine our own response is in the area of evolutionary theory. The famous Darwinian definition of nature as 'red in tooth and claw' is a construct on the evidence. The idea of nature developing and changing as it adapts to its environment making it possible for species to emerge does not require such a gloomy view of the natural world. From our own experience of its life, its beauty, its sense of freedom and its ability to flourish in the face of many different circumstances we might want to view nature in an entirely different way without going back on the evolutionary story.

One of the consequences of taking the Christian story seriously is a resistance to allowing the constructs of other less liberating views to shape our minds and so our culture. That was what St Paul was driving at when he warned the Colossian Christians, 'See to it that no one takes you captive through philosophy and empty deceit, according to human tradition, according to the elemental spirits of the universe, and not according to Christ' (Colossians 2:8). Clearly Paul was addressing particular challenges to the church in those days from alternative world views and constructs. The point is not to encourage a sort of intellectual imperialism by Christians – hardly a possibility in these early years of a tiny and socially insignificant church. It is simply to prevent the mind of the church being corrupted by the imperialism of other world views. In effect Paul is saying, 'Your faith and experience of Christ give you a truthful and liberating way of seeing and experiencing the world as it is. Don't sell that and return your minds to a form of slavery.'

The vision of God

From whatever direction Christians come they are united in the sense of God unfolding the essential meaning of love. A vision of God is a way into discovering an eternal and indestructible being of love which is the secret of all reality. The love discovered in the being of God is the opposite of a narcissistic love turned in on itself. It is a love which creates, sustains, redeems, enables and liberates.

The bond between true love and freedom is in the heart of the being of God. There is an ontological freedom which is the spring from which all true freedom arises. 'If the Son shall make you free, you will be free indeed' (John 8:36). In the negative that is expressed as, 'perfect love casts out fear' (1 John 4:18). The vision of God which draws humanity on in the unfolding of our journey is one which liberates as it opens up the meaning of love. Freedom, therefore, is not a hope which we cling on to against the powerful forces of repression, both internally in the human spirit and externally in our culture, without any confidence in its truth. It is a description of the fundamental reality of existence. In God is true freedom because God is eternal and true love.

Such freedom is not isolation and anarchy. It is not licence and corruption. Anarchy and licence are both forms of servitude. Freedom is not the unbridled pursuit of individual pleasure and self-interest. That too is the road to social collapse and to tyranny. Freedom springs out of wholesome relationship. It is the outcome of love. It is the expression of love both in the human person and in the growth of human community. That vision which sustains us in the profound difficulty of making this real, even in the smallest of ways, is rooted in our understanding of the universe in relation to the divine being.

We deal in mysteries. The development of the Christian doctrine of the Trinity early in the life of the Church has given shape and form to the way Christians across the generations have sought to understand the universe. The doctrine holds to a powerful dynamic between the being of God and the being of our humanity. The oneness of God was kept from solitariness and the threeness spoke of the eternal reality of love, life and relational being in the heart of the divine person. Above all Trinity made possible the redemption of our humanity and the hope of the transformation of creation through the liberating power of God's love. The ultimate story of resurrection triumph over death and all the forces which do us down comes to pass in a way which affirms the dignity of our own being. It runs with the grain of the human journey for freedom. Victory is not at our expense but a coming together of our journey with the gospel hope of resurrection life and new creation.

If at the heart of all being is a living and powerful dynamic of love and freedom, then creation has to be seen in that setting. Mechanistic views cannot be made to work. The universe is not some piece of divine engineering run by a rule book. Nor, indeed, are human beings to be seen in this way. The world is a living organism set free by the love of God to be in its own right and so are the people who inhabit it. This way of understanding God's work could be described as risk. It is better to see the risk as the meaning of divine love in action. How else can things come to be if a liberating selfless creative love drives the heart of all being?

The amazing range of the possibilities of the development of the universe and the particular growth of human experience are not an accident nor the careless act of fatalistic forces at war with each other. They are the outcome of the consistent and selfless love which is the secret of the meaning of our universe and of our lives within it.

One of the things which true love does is to let go. Parents have to let their children go. Holding on to them is a denial of creation and of love. It may seem a risk but it is the inescapable consequence of love. The relationship can only flourish where love gives space for the integrity of the other to exist and to grow. Love and domination cannot co-exist.

The idea of the divine love letting the universe go so that it may exist and grow in its own integrity is a result of attending to the vision of God. There can only be relationship where love enables space for the integrity of that which has come to be. If we want to understand that in the being of God, we can see it in the mystery of the relationship of the Son to the Father expressed in the freedom with which the Son accepts the journey of suffering and of the cross. This is not an imposed journey but one accepted and carried through because of the eternal bond of love and freedom within the heart of God. This is the painful work of love seen in the agony of the garden scene. 'Father, if it be possible let this cup pass from me. Nevertheless, not my will but yours be done' (Luke 22:42). We can see this as the risk that the divine enterprise might not be accepted. Or we can see it as the way love in freedom works – casting out fear and enabling responsible and costly action to happen.

If the universe and human life within it have been set free in relationship and given integrity by the creative act of love in freedom the consequences need to be considered. One of them concerns how we talk about the presence of God.

It is possible that God may have to be seen as absent if love is to fulfil its creative purpose. Presence can be denial of the liberty and integrity of the other. So Christian thought will have to come to terms with the idea of the absence of God and of the silence of God if it is to make sense of the presence of God and the Word of God. These themes are not unknown to the Bible. The picture of the relationship of Job to God in the book that bears his name is not one of abiding presence constantly intervening but of distance, of silence and even of absence. The love God has for his servant Job is not in doubt. But God does not deal directly with Job until the last scene of the book. There is a divine conversation with

Satan in which God is confident in Job's capacity to respond
to the destructive forces of evil which launch themselves on
Job and his household. Job is left in freedom to grow through
even these ghastly experiences. From Job's point of view God
is absent and silent.

'If I go forward, he is not there;
    or backward, I cannot perceive him;
on the left he hides, and I cannot behold him;
    I turn to the right, but I cannot see him.
But he knows the way that I take;
    when he has tested me, I shall come out like gold.'

(Job 23:8–10)

Christian thought has had quite a struggle wrestling with
the character of the presence of God in the universe. One
of the contemporary ways is to focus on the work of the Spirit
creating possibilities and opening space for freedom. A sort
of panentheism has taken root in Christian thought.[11] God is
not to be wholly identified with creation – pantheism. God
is, however, to be seen permeating the living order of the
universe – the source of its energy and life.

There is clearly some important truth to this. It is, after all,
the New Testament which speaks of freedom being discovered
where the Spirit is to be found. That sense of an open universe
engaging with the being of God rescues us from reductionism
and determinism. The interplay of divine life and the ongoing
creativity of the universe cannot be predicted. It is open and
full of surprise. The same is true of human living both personal and social. There is a wonder in the openness of the
future. That must have something to do with the mystery of
the divine action in the world.

Nevertheless this needs counterbalancing with the proper
Christian experience and truth of the God who is other and
distant and even absent. That can be presented in the false
way of suggesting God's lack of concern for the world – a
sort of divine imperialism which refuses to get caught up in
the dirty business of life and its struggles. As with Job it can

feel like injustice. In the Christian tradition the absence of God is not about indifference but about space for freedom and growth in responsible life. We cannot move ahead unless we accept an obligation to live responsibly in freedom.

God is neither an interfering presence constantly checking up on how we are doing nor an endless stream of words giving us instructions on what decisions we must make. Love gives us space to learn to be what might be possible if we but catch the vision. We must, therefore, be careful about that sort of incarnational theology which has God there all the time. It may be important to say, 'not there'. After the resurrection the persistent message was, 'he is not here' (Mark 16:6). The risen Christ was more absent than present – gone ahead encouraging his disciples forward to a new set of obligations. Indeed, the story is about entrusting to them the task that comes from a conviction that Christ is risen. Dependency is broken and a new opportunity is created for freedom in responsible ministry.

We must similarly be careful about the sort of theology which has God constantly giving the people direction and instruction on what to do. There is a lack of confidence in the Church today which locks people into dependency upon direct revelation or worse the revelations offered to others. Beware those who come with direct words from God to direct others as to how to live their lives. We need to remember that because God has spoken with such effect and discipline in Jesus Christ there is no need of repetition. God has spoken and we must listen rather than go on seeking new words. The silence of God is crucial to the journey we have to make in the world. The point of the resurrection is to give us confidence to travel. In that we may well have a sense of the glory of God nearby and a deep sense of the abiding love of God sustaining us as we make some sense of the journey.

The distance of God is crucial to the flourishing of life in the universe. The silence of God is crucial to the flourishing of our culture. Both enable love to mean freedom. Freedom for the unfolding life of the universe to happen in unpredictable ways surprising us with new avenues of living. Freedom for humankind to develop social order and culture and to be surprised by the way the future leads into different forms of living for people. The constant interplay with the vision of God enables us to make the judgements which we cannot escape about what is good and bad, what is to be nurtured and what is to be left behind, how to undo the myths which threaten our integrity and the hope of liberty, and to give account of how we have made each part of the journey. The absence and the silence make for relationships and for the possibility of maturity.

We are at a point in our history when we need space for diversity. Just as the universe is creative of an amazing range of life and reality so human experience has manifest diversity and difference. That is certainly at the heart of the post-modern unease with modernity. The undergirding realities which enable such a kaleidoscope of experience to be held together in a creative moment of possibility can only emerge once we come to terms with the diverse character of our living. Far from being a threat to us it is full of the hope of growth and development.

This is symbolised for me in the contrasts of holiday travel in my childhood and today. In the summer of 1946 as a small boy I stood with my family on Waterloo Station waiting for the train to take us on holiday to the Isle of Wight. The station forecourt was packed and overcrowded as, it seemed, all of London and district was going on holiday. The crowd was predominantly British and certainly all white. It belonged to that period immediately after the war when it was possible for people from the professional classes and working classes to holiday together – the nation had had to hold together in war and now it felt together in the peace. It was a modern world looking for universal solutions to the macro problems of reconstruction after the war and of avoidance of any return to the depressive years of the 20s and 30s. A sense of one culture facing the future together. It was an illusion then but people believed it.

31

Today you have only to go to Heathrow Airport at holiday time to witness the change. Again great crowds of people waiting to be taken away on holiday – this time across Europe and wider afield. A multi-cultural community of people speaking many languages, believing different faiths and none, multiple in household and family structure and inhabiting a range of cultures, the like of which we knew only at a distance through our study of empire in 1946. A postmodern world in which the integrity of a multiplicity of human stories and cultures has to be encountered.

If we believe in a God who means love in freedom then the beginning of our response to this contemporary experience needs to be a confidence that love gives space for diversity to flourish. God can be at a distance and encountering our world without many words. If theology and the Church are to engage with this they must do so within the conviction that freedom means recognition of the integrity of creation and of human life. We stop going down the road of trying to impose a predetermined culture and start to enable the development of our own culture. In ways which make it possible for the world and human beings to flourish and grow. That is the struggle for liberty and the meaning of love.

If this is the meaning of the divine being for us then our response will have to include deeper contemplation of the vision of God, a growing sense of the community learning to listen in silence if it is to listen to the meaning of the diversity of our humanity, and a capacity to give space for the task of interpreting what is heard and seen. By such means not only do we promote the freedom for which creation was destined but we walk the road of community in diversity.

Creation and the Meaning of Freedom

The experience of being human involves the making of choices. The freedom we possess is not absolute. The freedom enjoyed by creation is relative to the mystery of the divine freedom. The choices we have to make are constrained by the environment we live in. Poverty, for example, is a great restraint upon people's choices. It does not, however, totally destroy the capacity to choose. The choice may well lie between staying where you are and hoping you can survive until the next crop is harvested or moving somewhere else where food might be more readily available for your family. Poor people and communities are constantly having to make such decisions. Part of being human is learning how to make choices even in the most restricted of circumstances.

Is the business of choosing an illusion? We experience choice but in reality it has no meaning. It is possible that the universe is random and without meaning. Our capacity to flourish and experience what might be called a good life is accidental. We are the victims of chance or even of fate. We must make the most of the present because we do not know what tomorrow will bring with it. In times of plenty we allow an immediate hedonism to shape our lives. In time of hardship we are exposed to despair and even to death. The way we see our lives sways from extreme to extreme according to what a random and meaningless world is doing to us. Our life is on a continual and unpredictable pendulum between pleasure and pain, despair and hope.

The division between those who believe that choice is real and that there is a genuine openness about the universe and those who hold to strongly deterministic ideas cuts across the

divide of faith and unbelief. A strong doctrine of predesti-
nation and the sovereignty of the Divine Will have left many
Christians with a sense that their life is predetermined and
but the setting for the unfolding of a higher purpose.[1] Both
modern genetic theory and cosmology have led the philosophers of science to wonder whether both the mystery of
the universe and the meaning of human life are wholly within
our grasp. What need of God when it is possible to conceive
a time when we will know how things happen in the universe
and why individuals live and behave as they do?[2] So either
through a doctrine of the sovereignty of God's purposes and
power or through a confidence in contemporary science to
deliver to us the full mystery of both the life of the whole
universe and the life of human beings the door begins to shut
on the sense of openness and freedom in the universe.

In the light of the history of both theology and of scientific
theory we might be forgiven for suggesting a 'yes, but'
response. The extremes of theological theories which crush
the liberty of the person under the all-powerful will of God
are a consequence of the abandonment of the paradoxes of
the biblical story for a rigorous application of secular ration-
alism and logic to the doctrine of God.[3] A certain sort of
logic runs away with systematic thought and ends on the
buffers of an idea that everything was determined before
anything began and there is nothing that can be done about
it. The theological version is in the doctrine of double pre-
destination – the decision about whether we go to heaven or
hell has already been made. The secular version is in a narrow
genetic theory which sees all of human life as the workings
of a genetic computer which one of these days we will be
able to read with full confidence.[4]

This 'yes, but' response makes good sense of the history.
Cosmology has moved, for example, beyond Newton. Evolutionary theory has developed well beyond Darwin.
Einstein's theory of relativity has revolutionised twentieth-
century science and moved it well beyond the rigid optimism
of Newtonian concepts. If the development of knowledge has

led to the introduction of the 'but' into what was thought to be certain in generations past are we not entitled to believe that there are still some surprises ahead which will introduce the 'but' into what many present as certain today? The critical question, raised from within our own experience, does not require us to go back on the journey of human understanding – that is the fundamentalist error. We are not required to deny the advances of human knowledge in cosmology and evolutionary theory. Rather there is a simple refusal to absolutise working theories. These are useful in opening up our understanding and progressing human knowledge. They are leading us on down a path which is still being travelled. An open understanding of reality is rooted in the conviction that it is neither possible nor desirable to try and predict or see the end of the road which we travel. Reticence about all things modern includes scepticism about theories made absolute by their proponents.[5]

The experience of both being human and living in the universe does not fit well with any theory which tries to lock up the future. We live on the paradox of human freedom and the unpredictability of the universe. We refuse to abandon hope and choice in the most extreme of circumstances and we are reticent about the arrogance which suggests that we are in control. Neither fatalistic determinism on the one hand nor anarchy on the other make sense of what we experience. The constructs we work with about the universe and about the shape and meaning of our humanity have to have some real connection with what we experience.

The freedom for love, which is at the heart of the Divine Being as revealed in the Christian story, both keeps our story open to the future and prevents its collapse into anarchy. Understandings of God are not, of course, dependent upon scientific fashion. Theories about the universe and its beginnings and about the structure of the human person neither require faith in God nor undermine it. If the Copernican revolution rescued science from the hands of theology it is important that we rescue theology from the dominance of science. The help that science and theology can give to each other is undermined by any sense of the dependency of one on the other. There is nothing in the Christian understanding of God which hinders the journey of discovery and the endeavour at understanding which is the driving force of modern cosmology and genetic science. Rather the Christian understanding is encouraging because it insists on an open understanding of reality and, therefore, expects the journey to continue to open up new truth and new understandings of reality. We cannot stop where we are and think the journey is over.

Christian belief and freedom in the cosmos

The shape of Christian believing can help us with the journey. It gives a construct on reality which makes sense of who we are and how we experience the world. The creative energy of the Divine Being springs from the essential meaning of God as Love working towards freedom. The eternal oneness of God is life and energy. The Trinity of Persons in the oneness of God is love creating freedom. All that is created out of such being has its own integrity to travel the way of love working for freedom. We must not, therefore, set God against the responsibility of having to decide and of making the journey for ourselves. The journey is to be made in com-munion and communion is freely entered into by those who choose to travel this way. So our freedom is a mirror of the meaning of the heart of God. We have, therefore, to choose how we understand the world of which we are a part. The construct we choose will affect the choices we make for the shaping of the future.[6]

The creativity implicit in the Christian understanding of God opens the way for a number of attitudes and approaches which might help us find our place in the world today.

Mystery in the universe

First, it opens up and affirms a sense of mystery in the human encounter with the universe. Mystery is rooted in a conviction that the meaning of the universe is rooted in God and in an acceptance of the boundaries of human perception. Such an approach encourages reverence rather than fear. The sheer scale of the outcome of the creative energy of love working for freedom deepens the sense of mystery in every person trying to understand the scale and complexity of the universe. Because there is confidence that what we encounter is for us rather than against us – good rather than evil – there is a confidence in approaching it. That confidence is critical to the development of human enquiry into the character of the universe. It is confidence rather than arrogance. Arrogance suggests the universe is for us – there to serve our chosen agendas. Confidence respects it for itself as something not only greater than our imagination but as something rooted in the creative power of the being of God. It is for us as a potential friend.

The outcome of such an approach will be evidenced in reverence of people in relating to the universe and their created environment. It does not exist for our immediate pleasure. It is to be treasured rather than exploited for our immediate needs. It is a potential partner and friend in enabling us fulfil the vocation of being human. Partly out of fear but also partly out of amazement at the sheer scale of the universe there is a growing sense of the importance of the way we relate to and care for the world which provides us with our home.

This sense of mystery helps us steer a path between the twin dangers of the wanton exploitation of the natural world on the one side and the idolisation of nature on the other. We can make consistent, if complex, choices with some confidence that the good path can be kept to. We cannot evade the responsibility of making choices either by worshipping nature or by simply viewing it as there for us to do what we will. Judgements have to be made and that is part of the formation of a mature and mutual relationship with the environment within which we live. Mystery leads to communion, friendship, respect and trusteeship – an acceptance of the obligation of responding to and caring for the natural world.[7]

Change in the universe

The second approach is a recognition of the diversity and the changing character of the world. Modern theories of the origin and nature of the universe point to it as a growing and expanding reality. It is always changing. The idea of a fixed and immutable sort of universe belongs to the understanding of a previous age. We live in a multi-faceted universe in which energy and matter, time and space all interact. It is not possible to predict how the universe will develop – whether it will cease to expand and then contract and draw back to its beginnings or go on growing without limit. In like manner the way evolution works is not predictable – the environmental conditions and the choices made feed into an ever-changing pattern of life. The capacity to adapt to the changing environment is the outcome of choices made.

This encourages us to see a parallel between the emerging life of our world and universe and the unknown future for the shape of human living. As St Paul said, 'Hope that is seen is not hope and we hope for what we do not see' (Romans 8:24–5). It is a text which might do duty for our contemporary journey of cosmology and genetic theory. Hope is rooted in a confidence that the journey is worthwhile and that what is discovered can help us. But it is a hope which looks for what is not yet seen and known.

A proper reticence about how much we know and see goes hand in hand with a conviction that truth and the meaning of things lie in the heart of God. The danger of knowledge is that it tempts human beings into acting like gods – we know and we have the power to take whatever action we like. The destroyers of our natural world behave like gods, thinking it a right to use what nature produces without restraint and outside the boundary of respect for the world as it is emerging. A sense of not knowing and of having to learn each step of the way makes for a healthy caution in what we do. Respect and caution need to be watchwords for a world under threat of massive human exploitation as it struggles to sustain its growing millions. We must hand on our natural world to the future generations so that they too can enjoy the surprises of the journey still to be undertaken. Room has to be made for the unseen future.

The strength of life

Third, we need to recognise the vibrancy of life and its choices. Far from seeing the world as a place of death and decay we need to see it as abounding in the possibility of life and that such life is encouraged by the choices that have to be made at all levels of reality. If we refuse to accept that the universe is a deterministic machine – a sort of macro pre-programmed computer, then life is delightfully free. We cannot determine what is to happen next. In that respect human life is no different. Thankfully, our future is not predictable and so not open to the exploitation of power. The endeavour of some to behave like gods is fraught with failure. The future surprises us and we find ourselves moving down avenues we did not know existed.

The national weather service told us, on 15 October 1987, that we had no need to worry, no storms were about to hit England. A local weather buff in the South-East sent in a weather report to his local paper saying the district was about to be hit by hurricane-force storms. The paper, anxious and not fully believing, printed the report. That night the country was hit by the worst storms for 300 years causing havoc and devastation across the South and East of England. The storms not only changed the visible landscape of the South, it also changed the life of that local weather man. From that time

39

on his whole career has been taken up with his work on the weather. From a part-time hobby it became the mainstay of his vocation. No one could have foreseen that change in one person's direction in life on 15 October 1987 and only the outworking experience in the subsequent years has made what was not known and seen known and visible. If that has been true of individuals caught up in the storm of 1987 it is certainly true of the natural world. Some surprisingly good things have come out of apparent disaster. The renewal and reshaping of the environment in South-East England has been the strongest where there has been the least intervention in the natural processes of recovery. The life of the world has its own integrity and human beings must work with it.

In other words a confident engagement with the world does not depend on us thinking that we are in control. It involves the more truthful, if more risky, business of accepting that we have to respond to the outcomes of the choices already made. We also have to live in response to the continuing vibrancy of the life of the world we share with other people and with the rest of the created order.

That leads to a deep love of all life and a desire to enable it, protect it and sustain it. We move with the character of the created order in enjoying the life of the world and in enabling it to flourish. Things move forward as life encounters life. There is a sense of freedom and of movement in the world. At all levels nature seeks to resist the forces of death and to enjoy the benefits of life. Even death works to serve the possibility of life for others.

The urgency of us learning again the primacy of life and our duty to sustain it does not need labouring in a world whose living environment is under such sustained attack. The massed bombers of the last World War have not done the damage to the world which human hands have perpetrated, in recent years, on the natural world. Human life suffers as a consequence of the uncontrolled and wanton destruction of the environment. The developed world is particularly wanton and a profound change of mind is required within it if the persistent damage done by the insatiable desire for ever-growing levels of material prosperity is to be reversed. The developed world needs to come alongside the developing world in tackling the issues of debt so that resources can be released to rescue the growing populations of the world from the damage done in the terrible business of trying to survive. It is no good the developed world complaining, for example, about the destruction of trees in Africa as people find wood for fuel to cook their food and keep their families warm when such nations are left without the resources to build both the confidence and the structures needed for a balanced and just life. Caring for people and caring for the environment go hand in hand. A commitment to fairness and inclusiveness in social life is the other side of the coin of environmental care. Greed and exploitation of people will be mirrored by the irresponsible exploitation of the natural resources of the world. A love of life leads to a desire for justice for all and a care of the world people live in.

In this the sense of the oneness of God goes hand in hand with a commitment to the interdependent character of the modern world. The journeys people make within it are multiple and ever changing but they are not isolated. We share a common inheritance and an undivided duty to nurture and sustain life for the benefit of all. A recognition that we not only have a duty to care for the world but are dependent upon it is paralleled by a sense that not only have we a responsibility for the well-being of others but we are also dependent upon their exercise of vocation. There has to be consistency between the way we relate to the environment and the way we seek to sustain the human community.

We are creatures too

Fourth, human beings are part of, not apart from, the whole environment in which we live. We are creatures as well. In the fundamental distinction of Creator and created we belong with the created order. Human life is made from the dust of

41

the earth and to that dust it returns when life is complete. Our commonality is not just with other human beings. There is a fundamental solidarity with the natural world and with the energy and diversity of a universe forever changing and adapting towards the future.

> I said in my heart with regard to human beings that God is testing them to show that they are but animals. For the fate of humans and the fate of animals is the same; as one dies, so dies the other. They all have the same breath, and humans have no advantage over animals; for all is vanity. (Ecclesiastes 3:18–19)

This solidarity of people with the rest of creation helps to define the way human beings exercise their gifts of intelligence and choice in relation to the rest of life. The concept of trusteeship and of stewardship, rooted in the Christian understanding, is not basically hierarchical: God at the top, humankind next down, then the animals and finally the green world. The trusteeship or stewardship is an exercise in responsible freedom for the well-being of the whole. We are in it together sharing a status as created life. That can be put in terms of self-interest – if we do not care for the world today it will not feed us tomorrow. Or it can be put in a more principled way – the flourishing of all life is one of the secrets of the meaning of human life if it is to flourish. The power of choice which is vested in our nature means that we can move towards destruction and death or towards life and freedom. The Christian vision encourages us to seek continually life and freedom and to resist the forces of death.

These choices are always contextual and unpredictable. The story is not one of the steady progress of the world towards utopia but of the constant need to respond to the present for the sake of the vision of love and freedom. The next steps on the way are always the critical ones. What can we do to begin to reverse the insatiable appetite of developed societies for the limited resources of the present? How can we help the poor of the world live with greater dignity and support

42

them in caring for their own environment? The vision which drives such practical deciding forward is the larger vision of a universe sustained by love which constantly enjoys life and opportunity. The outcomes are not predictable because the unfolding of the future involves the impact of the choices of others and of the movement of the whole environment. Doing the right thing, however, is not dependent on the guarantee of the outcome but on the truthfulness of the vision from which we construct our understanding of the world. Goodness, truth and beauty need no other justification than that of the nature of all being.

If human life is to be seen as having a solidarity with the whole natural order – creature sharing in the journey of the created – then we share with creation that belonging to a world rich in life and open in freedom to growth and change. In nature the living world is constantly adapting to its changing environment. Sadly, that sometimes leads to the extinction of species. The natural world changes. Human beings change. We express that in the changing cultures which are created for the management of our lives. Just as it is not possible to freeze nature and preserve it unchanged so it is neither possible nor wise for human beings to freeze culture and try and preserve it in the face of the changing demands of the environment. An agrarian society has different needs from an industrial one – a rural society is different from an urban one. These diversities do not have to destroy a sense of mutuality and shared life. They do require sensitivity to the different demands of different vocations and forms of social living. In all contexts the story moves on and, however wonderful it is perceived to be, we have to learn to let the past go and face the challenges and choices of the present.

Life on its way to extinction is life which has given up on the task of adapting to the challenges of its environment. To decide not to choose is a dangerous thing to do. To stop the journey is the first step to ending the journey. The absolute and unshiftable is in the heart of all being. It is an unbelieving world which absolutises the constructs of our human life. It

43

is the vision and the confidence born of the larger vision in the meaning of love, freedom, truth and goodness which gives the continuity and the unity.

That vision also provides the space to make the choices. Remove these undergirding and living absolutes and the world can become prey either to the fatalism of those who think they know or to an unprincipled anarchy in which everyone pursues their own goals and takes no care for the shared obligations of our life together. A postmodern world will fall apart and unwittingly hasten the further destruction of the environment unless it can find some sense of shared life across the diversities which have to be recognised and accepted.[8]

The vision of God neither moves with the heteronomy of a culture imposed from outside nor with the autonomy of isolated and self-orientated individualism. It holds in play the possibility of communion which is both affirming of an open and free world and the liberating experience of learning to live in solidarity with the rest of creation.

This is one of the great challenges of our time. A recovered sense of responsibility for the created order will not be achieved by the enforced order of governments but by a changed perception in the minds of people. Protecting the environment by inter-governmental agreements on the international stage may be important but success can only be achieved when people see their world as a friend and partner in the mystery of the journey of living. There is nothing in either cosmology or evolutionary theory to prevent us viewing our world and its life in such a framework of understanding. Keeping the universe open through a sense of the power of love working for freedom empowers us in the task.

The Holy Trinity and the Meaning of Autonomy and Community

Every generation has to work on the way to balance the demands of the rights of individuals with the needs of communities. A motorway, for example, needs a new service station. Whichever site is chosen will involve disruption to local people who will lose their land and have a busy road users provision intruding upon their community. The needs of the motorist versus the right of individuals to have their homes and land protected from unforeseen intrusion. It's a case study which could be repeated many times.

These sorts of dilemmas take us to the heart of the meaning of our humanity. Am I an isolated individual for whom community is a matter of choice – and society a construct of independent individuals? Or am I essentially a member of a human community with inescapable bonds with others? Is society something we construct or are we formed within the given communities from which our life arises? The question becomes more theological when we ask, 'is the conviction and experience of the individual person, formed and growing in the given relationships of community, part of the givenness – or gift – of life?' Christian thought has refused to give up on the double nature of the Christian understanding of the human. People are to be seen both in the integrity of their own individuality and as essentially and inescapably made within and for community. Christian thought refuses to be driven into having to choose between the individual and the community. It also resists the demand to give priority to one or the other.

This is an issue which has been at the centre of a considerable amount of philosophic debate in the twentieth century.[1]

The enormous strength of the corporate power of both the state and of large and monopolistic institutions has raised critical questions about the significance and protection of the individual. Trouble has arisen at both ends. We have witnessed the effects of a century of the abuses of state power in which individuals have been considered to be expendable in the interests of corporate ideology. We have also seen the way unfettered libertarianism has exposed vulnerable people to social abuse leading to the demand for corporate protection and help. Leaving the individual to fend for herself ends up with many individuals victimised and unprotected from the abuses of power.

The philosophic and political pendulum swings from generation to generation. Too much corporate intrusion on behalf of the 'people' and the demand for protection of the individual grows. In Western society we have been through two decades of witnessing the pendulum swing in the direction of the free individual. People should be free to pursue their chosen business with the minimum intrusion of corporate restraints possible. In the sphere of economic and social philosophy Hayek's work has been dominant and represents a swing away from the mid-century domination of J.M. Keynes.[2]

At the end of the Second World War decisions had to be made about the direction for the future. That required a judgement about the significance of our experience in the middle of the twentieth century. There were those who believed that having purged Europe of the Fascist nightmare democratic societies needed to use the modern corporate state for the welfare of the people and for the management of the economy so that we never again experienced the social, political and economic disasters of the 1920s and 30s. Keynes and Beveridge belonged in that tradition. Having developed the power of the state to overcome Hitler it seemed reasonable to use it to build a new social and democratic peace. Others feared the growing power of the state would both cripple enterprise and threaten the essential freedoms of decent human life. The state needed containment. Hayek saw things more in that direction.

In the sphere of political philosophy the debate between John Rawls – defending a concept of social justice as that which we would choose if we were innocent of the outcomes of our history – and Robert Nozick whose deep distaste for corporate power is rooted in a clear commitment to the liberty of the person.[3] These are two very contrasting visions of the meaning of human life in the world. Rawls believed in the social contract freely accepted, Nozick in the fundamental freedom of the individual constantly threatened by the heteronomous society. Both are picking up, in the late twentieth century, on the seventeenth-century debates about the nature of the social contract – is the power of the state rooted in the need for power or in a contract which preserves the essential integrity of the rights of individuals?[4]

These twentieth-century versions of the endeavours of Hobbes and Locke to find the philosophic roots of the political community and of the relationship of the individual to it illustrate the persistence of the basic issue. The violence and divisions of the seventeenth century lay at the root of their thinking. In the face of the naked realities of power what sort of contract gave foundation to the state and how was the individual to be related to it? The violence and abuses and inequalities of the twentieth century are at the root of our debate.

That debate will continue! In a pluralistic society of many cultures and faiths and of none, of many different lifestyles and self-chosen ways of living, the human story, the question of what holds life in common, if anything, becomes critical. Are we simply left with a postmodern diversity in which we ought to stop even thinking and trying to find the bonds of community across the range of our human experience? Perhaps it does not matter and we should simply all get on with living as we choose.

Yet there is plenty of evidence in our history to warn us against such a casual approach. The wrestling of the philosophers of our time with these issues is not just a matter of idle academic games but the response to deep fears and concerns for human well-being. Failing to attend to the roots of our common life may lead in directions which eventually will threaten to destroy the liberty of a plural society. If peace is not held by a sense of the common bonds of life in the universe and of life between people it may well only be held by those who win the power and hold on to it by the sword. Both individuals and different communities have an investment in unity. The flourishing of diversity and the providing of room for individuality is dependent upon a sense of common life. The eternal questions, 'Am I my brother's keeper?' and 'Who is my neighbour?', provoke answers crucial to the health of our life in society. The Old Testament answer, in the story of Cain and Abel, is that God expects one brother to guard the life of the other (Genesis 4). The New Testament answer to the question of neighbour is implicitly inclusive and universal. Your neighbour is whoever needs your support irrespective of who they are and where they come from. All should receive a neighbourly care (Luke 10:29–37).

God as one

The roots of these responses in the Bible are in the nature and being of God. The Scriptures are at one in holding to the conviction that there is but one God. In a world dominated by many gods – the gods of the nations – the covenant conviction of the Old Testament is that these are no gods. The idols and the cultic sanctuaries are empty of true spiritual life and power. The gods on display are but constructs of wood and stone (Isaiah 44:9–20). They have no power in reality. God is essentially one and 'other'. God is not creature but creator. The confines of the created orders cannot contain the one true God who is other. The holiness – or otherness – of God speaks of the fundamental difference between the nature and being of God and the nature and being of the world. God is God. God cannot be contained and controlled by the religious practices of idolatry or by the human endeavour at naming the divine being.

All life and being, all reality comes from the life and being of the one true God who is other than us. Jewish, Islamic and Christian faith all affirm this essential truth. The Old Testament is distinguished by this vital conviction about the nature of God and the one God who is the creator and redeemer of all. There is no other. Whatever differences there are between the creeds of Judaism, Islam and Christianity – and some of the distinctions are deep and complex – their root is common. Together they believe in the one God and resist all idolatries. The temptation to yield to the human desire to make gods to suit our needs or so to name the gods that they serve our purposes is persistent in the story of the unfolding of the biblical faith. Even more persistent is the prophetic response to guard the essential truth that the God who is revealed as the redeemer of the people and who enters covenant with the people is the one true and only God.

The religion which flows from this truth has resisted all stories and beliefs which threaten to compromise that conviction. In the Old Testament the corruption of the covenant faith in idolatry and cultic abuse draws the wrath of the prophets because it brings the one true God down to the level of the gods of the nations who are no gods. God is not one god among many. In the New Testament and in the history of the early Church a gnostic dualism, which saw the universe as subject to the heavenly struggle between good and evil, had to be set aside for the conviction that there is only one Lord – the God and Father of our Lord Jesus Christ. The vision of God which Paul expounds in the Colossian Letter is rooted in the tradition of the Old Testament. The fullness of this God has taken residence in Jesus Christ.

This sense of the uniqueness, oneness and holiness of God has clear consequences for human understanding and living. The endeavour, for example, in which religion is a construct of human life for the meeting of our needs or the justification of our institutions is utterly false. However subtly put, true religion is not about how we manipulate God for our own ends. That is what idolatry is all about. In a similar way the conviction about the nature of God exorcises any view of reality which sees human life caught up in a universe which is in effect a spiritual battleground between the forces of God and those of evil. Whatever we judge to be the reality of the power of evil we cannot present the world as dualistic. God is Lord and even the mysterious forces of the spiritual orders are subject to the divine life.

This conviction creates a sense of confidence in us that the world and our lives, which have their origin in the creative and redemptive act of God, can have a unity and consistency which lead to growth rather than disintegration. We can engage with one another in hope and with the possibility for good. The otherness of God is not to be equated with any sense of an indifference in God. The biblical idea has no place for notions of the gods living apart and treating the world as a sort of playground. What the holiness of God reminds us of is that the relationship we have with God is one of creature to Creator, of redeemed to Redeemer. It is the relationship of the loved to Love.

That bond is expressed in the sense of the goodness of creation and in particular in the notion of the divine image in human beings. There is nothing to be afraid of in the world we inhabit. Its life arises out of the heart of the being of Love in Freedom. The characteristic of the Divine Life is stamped on the life of the created order. Down the centuries this has been expressed in a variety of ways. A more static view of the universe, which was held to in Newtonian times, led to an emphasis upon the order of the universe – it worked to established laws and had a sense of purpose. We could trust it. Everything had its place and purpose. The danger of such thinking was to encourage the view that we could gain control of the world. Once we understood the laws of nature (or the ways of Providence) the world became our subject. The idea of God might be needed at the start but theology could soon be dispensed with since things worked to immutable laws. The world and the universe worked to known laws and we were now in charge. Trust in a world rooted in the mystery of Divine Life shifted to trust in the work of science and of cosmology. With Newton on one side and Darwin on the other giving us control of both the cosmos and the origins of life, what need had we of God?

The revolution in science brought about by Einstein and by contemporary understandings of cosmology and of quantum theory make such images of ordered life more difficult and less pertinent than once they seemed. The universe is not a great machine which now runs smoothly according to its own inner energy. It is an expanding ever-changing reality in which energy and matter, time and space are all interdependent. Its future path and that of its constituent parts have an unpredictability about them which makes for a sense of openness and growth. The confidence we have must be based on an understanding of freedom as hope and possibility in love.

The fundamental point remains – people can engage with this reality with confidence. That confidence is an act of faith. It is faith which is consonant with the long and consistent tradition, expressed in the faith of the Old Testament, about the nature of reality seen in the light of our experience of God. This provides a strong foundation for the scientific enterprise. People who view the world as dangerous and hostile defend themselves from it and stay out of it. Primitive tribes who looked upon the outside world as inhabited by the gods could only enter that world via ritual processes of protection. In general people do not believe in a space wars understanding of the universe. It is not a playground for mysterious hostile powers. It is open for us to investigate and learn and wonder. That understanding of God, which we find in the Scriptures, is entirely consonant with this approach. We can have confidence in the universe.

In relation to the perplexing questions of human community which are of such critical importance to the modern world these convictions bring a similar confidence for the practical business of building peaceful and free societies. We can accept that the bonds of life which bring people together are deeper than the diversities. The differences between people come from the enormous range of experiences which they have in their daily lives and cultures. Our social and personal environment makes for a wonderful range of experience of what it means to be a person living in community.

What we share together in the meaning of our humanity, however, is of much greater significance to us than the divergent paths we find ourselves exploring. Every endeavour at dividing humanity and fitting it into some socially useful hierarchy has not only been utterly disastrous but persistently resisted as untrue to our basic human nature. The disasters have been seen in our own time with every form of racism and the abuses and genocides which follow on from it. The resistance is witnessed in the constant crumbling of these artificial borders as human friendship and love and the common desire for freedom bring broken communities together. These experiences require us to make important choices of conviction. Which story of human life do we trust? Is the story evidenced by those who protected Jewish people in the face of the Nazi terror and who struggled across the racial divide against apartheid in South Africa? Or is it the story of racial superiority and of the division of humanity into forever separated groups? The twentieth century has answered. Racism may be all too alive and well. But the Nazi terror has been defeated and the story of the brave few was the story of the future. Apartheid came crashing down – the great edifice had feet of clay and when hope seemed so far away for its victims it cracked and fell. Those who fought it across the racist divide were the people who pointed to a more hopeful future.

The story of the essential bonds of a common life across the divergences of our humanity is entirely consonant with the biblical statement that human beings are made in the image of God. We share a common nature and a sense of oneness at the heart of our being. As God is one so humanity has an essential unity of being.

God as Trinity

In Christian faith the understanding of God is taken a stage further than the simple but crucial conviction of the oneness and otherness of God. This is a point of difference and controversy with our Jewish and Muslim brothers and sisters. The Christian community affirms that God may be described as three Persons in one God. We are a Trinitarian faith. For Christians that does not in any way compromise the essential truth about the unity and oneness of God. Nor does it, in the understanding of incarnation, compromise the sense of the otherness and holiness of God. The Christian faith in God is not one which requires us to believe in three gods nor, in the generality of creation or the specificity of the incarnation, to believe in some form of pantheism – the muddling of the being of God with creation.

The doctrine of the Trinity is the Churches' endeavour at making sense of the revelation of God, especially in the work and person of Jesus Christ. The language and thought forms of our human life are stretched to the limits to make known what humankind has witnessed in the revelation of God to the world in Jesus Christ. A number of important statements come together in this truth. 'Jesus is Lord' was the first credal statement made by the first Christians (Philippians 2:11). They had witnessed Jesus as risen from the dead and this confirmed to them that he was the one promised in the Old Covenant to be Messiah and Saviour. The wonder of God, evidenced in the Law and Prophets, is seen in all its beauty in Jesus Christ. The full meaning and character of the love which is at the heart of God's being is working among us in Jesus Christ. These convictions led on to a sense that, in a unique way, Jesus came from God to us. The Word was made flesh.

The encounter of humanity with Jesus Christ is personal – a bond of love grows between the eternal love in the heart of God and the heart of our being. In Jesus Christ there is a coming together of the being of God in love and the heart of human life. In that encounter is the promise of the transformation of our humanity. The doctrine of Trinity is set against all reductionism which tries to contain what is seen and experienced of God in Christ. Reductionism is in the assertion that Jesus is nothing more than a man. Or again, it might be suggested that Jesus is just a great religious leader. No particular divine purpose is to be discerned in his life and teaching. What Christian faith resists in these statements is the 'nothing more than' aspect of them. Trinity opens the door to the promise that in Jesus we have encountered the living God in the eternal Son. The Christ is in the heart of God from before all time and beyond the boundaries of creation. In Jesus creator and created are united. The Word made flesh. So we see God as Divine Person in the Son.

In the Son, as in the whole dynamic of revelation and of creation, we are witnesses to the creative energy of the Spirit of God – distinct and free and the one in whom the new life of God's love and freedom is brought to bear upon the world. This encounter is in no less a degree a personal relational encounter with God. Again, the doctrine of the Trinity keeps open the door to a widened imagination as to the meaning of the divine life in the work of the Holy Spirit. This is not a-personal but deeply touching the bond between the Divine Being in love and our being. This is how creation and Creator are united.

So the one God who is other than us is experienced through the extraordinary events of the appearance of Jesus Christ as a mystery of three Persons – a living energetic, eternal communion of love always creative of the future as of the past and present. One God in three Persons. The doctrine is sharp at the edges in what it stands against and subtle and imaginative in what it reveals of our experience of God. It stands against any reduction of the mystery of the divine life in Jesus by the Spirit. It stands against any positivism about human life and the created orders which threaten to reduce us to determinism or fatalism. It holds the world and the meaning of God open to the exploration of the meaning of love creative and energetic in the business of setting us free. In God is love not isolated and alone but a joyful communion in eternity of persons. In God is love not closed in on itself in a distant world of religious narcissistic pleasure but a creative energy creating new things, drawing existent things within its orbit and always opening up the future in hope.

The contemporary debate

Serious Christian thought is always moving between these reflections of faith and the daily experience we have of the present. As we do this so we find that the faith we have received through the revelation of God in Christ is entirely at one with our understanding and experience of the world as an environment in which we can pursue our human journey in confidence and hope. Such faith offers ways of seeing and understanding our life in community which encourage us on in the journey of goodness and truth.

When we return from this exploration of a truth at the heart of our Christian tradition to the immediate issues of the balance of the individual and the community, and of the management of a world of plural and diverse cultures and communities, we can begin to see the interplay of truth with experience. The edges are sharp in resisting those forces which would reduce the possibility of our humanity. The harder the pendulum is swung in the direction of unfettered individualism at the expense of a sense of communion and its obligations with others we begin to find a disjunction between what we are affirming and the central nature of reality as we have received it from the gospel. The harder the pendulum is swung in the other direction requiring individuals and small communities to yield to the corporate demands of cultural or political power again the greater the sense of moving outside the boundaries of love and goodness. Neither isolated and selfish individualism nor enforced social conformity fit well with the symbolic and powerful image of the one God who is open and creative love in three Persons.

If human life reflects in its own integrity the meaning of God – created in the divine image – then we will always be seeking for community rooted in the freedom which springs out of the heart of love. Whatever community we are considering – be it the household, or the community of vocation and work, or the artistic community, or the neighbourhood community, or the national community – the vision for which we strive is one of relationships rooted in the love which makes for liberty. Individuals begin to flourish where there is the stability of love. This is a basic truth which all families know and seek to make their aim. Members flourish and grow as persons in their own right when the stability of love offers them space to live in mutual relationships with the others in the home. The same truth is worked out appropriately for its context. The sharp edge is clear. The physical, emotional and sexual abuse of children in the home is beyond the boundary of the meaning of a loving community. The exploitation of a workforce in a corporate enterprise is outside the boundary. The oppression of peoples, races and communities by those who have political power is well beyond the limits of the meaning of human life lived in creative communion.

Inside the boundary there is plenty of room for imaginative development. The shape of the Christian mind formed in worship and contemplation of the divine mystery made known to us in Christ does not give a fixed blueprint of how we are to order our lives. We have to make these judgements for ourselves. As with the universe so with human life it is always changing and opening up new possibilities. The responsibility for working out how to live rests with those directly involved. The household has to consider for itself how the striving for a loving community is to be ordered. Each place in each culture will be different. There is a danger of creating a hierarchy of culture in which those on the fringes of power are judged by those at its heart. This can be as true in the Church as in the wider community. Normative cultures emerge which have more to do with people's desire for certainty than with the truth of what makes for good human life. By such means we escape the responsibility of having to work on the significance of our faith in the setting of our vocation. By such means we try to shut the door on the possibility of something new emerging in our experience. It is the faith in interplay with living which reveals boundaries.

There are many ways in which individuals and societies can bond with each other. We can learn as we make our own journey from the strengths and weaknesses of what others have found. One of the tasks of a complex society such as ours is to find ways of interrelating different experiences of being persons in communion with others. Not only is there a need for a recognition that people do live in many different community contexts but to find lines of commonality between them. Is it so surprising, for example, that people have difficulty establishing stability in their domestic lives if the values and cultures of other areas of their living are alien to such a desired outcome? The disjunction between working life and home life has been a serious problem in our society. If in the one setting competitive attitudes lead people to measure success in short-term notions of profitability, how hard it will be to adjust to a co-operative and shared community where service and sacrifice are the secret values for building lasting bonds of love and mutuality. People find it very hard to make connections between different environments. The complexity and diversity of the demands made on us today require some common values and visions to hold our lives together. Stress is often the result of a sort of cultural schizophrenia – people crack under the pressure of having to be different persons in different settings.

The world need not be a threat to us. Its meaning and our meaning can be rooted in a vision of God who is one and other and who in the beauty of the unity is an eternal experience of love between persons. This serves to strengthen our confidence to strive for a consistent and humane balance between our need for a clear sense of our own identity and our need for love and being loved. We must know who we are and we must share who we are with others especially with others who have lived a different story to our own.

On such a field as this the rich diversity of our culture becomes more opportunity than threat. Genuine communities of faith inhabit the range of human experience. The universality of the faith is not to be expressed in conformity to a transient religious culture but in the enabling of all people, in the multiple settings of our human journey, to find help and grace in discovering the boundaries of freedom in love. The sense of the world being rooted in the being of God, who is love working for freedom, keeps our sense of history and of the cosmos open. The constructs within which we live are not absolute. There is room for choice. Choice requires us to decide on our values. Values arise out of vision. It is not the specific choices our own history and culture require of us that should cause us concern. Rather it is the threat of cultural imperialism which should keep us alert. For Christians, the understanding of God expressed in the doctrine of Trinity is fundamentally moving against all cultural imperialisms. It insists on keeping history open and on the continuance of all our journeys from wherever we come.

If that vision gives people greater confidence not to give up on the journey towards the building of communities which enable persons to grow and flourish it will serve to strengthen us in the face of the tyrannies of corporate power and of unfettered anarchy. However difficult our immediate circumstances we seek for a better way and we seek to give that shape and form within the contemporary meaning of our life. That means the task is persistent. The journey must go on.

Section II

Politics, Postmodernism and Faith

Three contentious political issues raise the question of truth in a particularly sharp way for those concerned for the meaning of God. Human beings are engaged in a persistent struggle against the powerful drive to short-cut the divisions and conflicts of the world by oppressive and imposed orders of politics. That resistance requires a fresh construct of politics in the face of the challenges of diversity. In Europe, in Jerusalem and in Ireland we confront three case-studies of the dilemmas and threats of politics in a postmodern age. All have a religious dimension not too far beneath the surface.

Out of a study of these issues come themes which might inform all our management of conflict and of difference. These raise critical questions for faith. The humanising power of the love which liberates is on trial and at work in these matters. Getting it wrong is dangerous for the peoples caught up in the dilemmas and threatens disaster for faith communities tempted into popular but corrupt constructs of the meaning of God for the divided stories of our time.

Jerusalem – Nightmare or Vision

Making a pilgrimage to Jerusalem today can be one of the most sobering of all experiences. Of course, it is possible to visit the city, see the sites, contemplate on the sacred places, and be almost totally blind to the tragic dynamic of the city today. A pilgrim, however, who learns to reflect on the meaning for the present of the religious events to which the city bears witness, is confronted by all the complex and baffling questions of faith. Is there hope for the future? Can faith be a partner of such hope or will it be a hindrance? Jerusalem is a critical challenge to those who believe it possible for peoples with conflicting histories and beliefs to live together creatively in peace, freedom and justice. It also bears witness to a pivotal issue for religion – must religion always serve power and so deepen division?

Everywhere in Jerusalem the history is dominant. From the strange meeting of Abraham with Melchizedek (Genesis 14:17–20) through to the division of the city and the modern struggle for its identity, represented in the 1967 war, Jerusalem has witnessed life-transforming events. This is David's city to which he brought the Ark of the Covenant (2 Samuel 6:1–5). It is Solomon's city where the first temple was built (1 Kings 6). It is Hezekiah's city with the story of the survival of the Assyrian siege and the building of the water conduit and pool (2 Kings 18–20). It is the city which fell to the Babylonian hordes in Jeremiah's day – as Jeremiah said it would (2 Kings 24–5). It is the city of hope to which the people returned after the exile. It is Nehemiah and Ezra's city, with the rebuilding of its walls and temple.

This is the city to which Jesus came. He came as a boy with

his parents and he impressed the religious leaders with his wisdom even in these years of his youth (Luke 2:41–52). As he approached Jerusalem for the final confrontation the sight of the city moved him to tears. The paradox, between the deep significance it had in the mystery of God's covenant and it becoming the city of the rejection of his mission, deeply affected him (Luke 19:41f.). This paradox has a strongly theological note – Jerusalem is the city both of the crucifixion and of the resurrection, of death and of life, the city of condemnation and of hope.

It is the city which the Romans sacked and desecrated. They not only tore down the city but destroyed the Temple which has never been rebuilt. Jerusalem was a vital centre for the early Church. Paul came to this city to argue the case for the Gentile mission – a critical battle to be won if the message of Jesus was not to be restricted to becoming a sect of Judaism (Acts 15). The road which led to his eventual martyrdom started in Jerusalem (Acts 21:27ff.).

When Christianity became the dominant religion of the late Roman Empire Jerusalem took on a new significance. It became a place of pilgrimage. The Church of the Holy Sepulchre was built and a sense grew of the importance of the city as the location where the events which founded the Church had taken place. It became a city of pilgrimage.

Then in the seventh century Jerusalem was caught up in the rise and spread of Islam. It is the city of Muhammad to which, according to the story as recorded in the Koran,[1] he was transported at night from Mecca by the angels and from which he ascended to heaven. The site of the Dome of the Rock marks the point and lays a crucial foundation to the Islamic claim to be the true inheritor of the promise of Abraham. It is the city of the Dome of the Rock.

It became a city of religious war and conflict. The Muslims conquered it in the seventh century and held it thereafter. This is the city of the Crusades and of Saladin the Magnificent. For brief periods the Christian crusaders captured the city and sought to re-establish a Christian identity. The relics of their endeavours are still to be seen in the Holy Land. Jerusalem has long been a city of conquest and counter-conquest.

As we approach the modern era the city has been caught up in the Zionist cause. It is the city to which the growing Zionist movement in the late nineteenth and twentieth centuries aspired. In the twentieth century and most especially post 1948 with the division of Palestine and the de facto establishment of the State of Israel Jewish people have come from all over Europe to make their life in this land. Their aspirations are fixed on Jerusalem which is central to their hopes. Many long for the day when it will be seen by the world as Israel's capital city. Culturally, the city today is the city of religious Jews, Christians and Muslims. The historic division of the Old City into Christian, Muslim and Jewish sectors speaks of its cultural pluralism. It should be remembered that it is also the city of the modern secular person as well. Many of the Jews who have established their home here are secular Jews. What is indisputable is that Jerusalem is a divided and disputed city. It is a place of persistent political struggle between Jew and Palestinian. Three religions and two peoples claim the city for themselves. It is a deeply paradoxical and troubling place.

This city which ought to speak of peace has become a sign and symbol of the divisions and disharmonies of the twentieth century. It is in danger of becoming a battleground between partial and sectarian interests. It lives on the border between beauty and brutality.

The pilgrim is always struck by its beauty. Sitting on hills the ancient city is testimony to the way faith has inspired the creation of its walls and streets, churches, mosques and synagogues which are a pleasure to the human eye. The perceptive pilgrim is also struck by its brutality. Blood has been shed across the centuries of its history. Blood continues to be shed as its status remains a point of deep contention at the end of the twentieth century. Bombs continue to blow up buses and markets leaving a trail of death, bitterness and grief. This is not a city at ease with itself but one living in tension all the time. The footsteps of soldiers and the weapons of war which have been so much in evidence in its history are still all too visible on its streets today.

The divisions are complex and changing. It would be far too simple to tell the story as one of unresolved division between the three great monotheistic religions – the faith of Jewish, Muslim and Christian people. In like manner there is a limit to the story which sees the whole issue as the struggle between Palestinian and Jewish people. These religious and political issues might give us the outlines of a map. The detail is subtle and baffling. Jerusalem is disputed territory. The Israelis conquered it in 1967 but the world has not accepted as de jure what conquest has made de facto. The political status of Jerusalem will be the most troublesome part of the peace process (if that process continues). That political dispute needs to be distinguished from the long history of cultural and religious pluralism in the region. There have been deep cultural battles alongside the political struggles.

The Christian story can hardly be described as one of harmony and peace. The Holy Land has been a place of battle between Latin and Greek Christians. The deep division between Western and Eastern Christian traditions has left its mark on the history of this city. The Crusades inspired by the medieval papacy encouraged the crusaders to attack the churches of the East as well as the Muslim rulers of Palestine. The Crusades did permanent and irreparable damage to the way the Islamic rulers had provided for the resident Christian communities. They also served to confirm the historic divide of Eastern and Western Christianity.

These theological and apocalyptic divisions continue. In the twentieth century fundamentalist Christians, funded mainly by American groups, have attached their hopes for the future return of the Lord to the Zionist cause and the return of the Covenant people to Israel. The return of the Jews to the Promised Land is seen as fulfilment of biblical prophecy and a sign that we are living near the end times. A premillennial fundamentalism allied to right wing American politics has added another dimension to the confused religious history of this city. This has caused deep distress to the Palestinian Christians who trace their own life in the Church back to the earliest years of the gospel story in Palestine. Down the centuries in Crusades and in sectarian fundamentalisms Jerusalem has seemed to attract the divided and deviant forms of Christianity. The Church resident in the land has been the sufferer of these battles and ideologies brought from outside and has been abused by powerful interests within.

The story has its positive side – resurrection hope following crucifixion. The political changes of the twentieth century leading up to the difficulties of the present time have served to bring Christians together in the Holy Land and in Jerusalem. There is much deeper good will and a sense of sharing a common journey among the predominantly Palestinian Christian community. The considerable pressure upon the local churches has brought Christians closer to one another. In the face of the onslaught of the post 1948/1967 development of the State of Israel Christians have been motivated to co-operate and work together. This has taken place against a steady draining away of the life of the Church as Palestinian Christians have been either driven out of their homeland or have left to set up a new life in less troubled circumstances. The survival of the historic witness of the Church which can trace its history back to Jesus is dependent on solidarity in the face of the difficulties as yet unresolved. The work of the Middle East Council of Churches and of the networks created by agencies such as SABEEL[2] have been critical in creating this commonality of purpose. Nevertheless the history is one of division and of complexity which belie simplistic analysis.

The same bewildering complexity is to be found in the Jewish and Islamic cultures. The struggle between secular and religious Judaism has been a feature of the political and social history of the State of Israel. A visit to the Wailing Wall to see Jewish people at prayer makes it hard to believe that the Zionist vision was of a secular state. The secular origins of Israel is a fact often forgotten by pro Zionist Christians so intent on finding theological meaning in the return of the Jewish people to Israel. The Zionist vision is essentially political and cultural rather than theological and religious. There is a danger that fundamentalist groups will be used for immediate political ends by Israel with no real interest in the religious issues which are at the heart of these Christian sectarian concerns.[3]

Western Christians have much work to do to gain a truthful insight into the world of Islam. Crude and imperialist images of the faith of Islam will need to be cleared away if we are to begin to understand the diverse mind and inner struggles of that community of faith as it too tries to make sense of the unresolved issues of Palestine and the Middle East. If there is to be a critical engagement with the political outlook of Islamic society then the demonising tendencies of Western approaches to Islam will have to give way to an intelligent understanding. Confrontational images play straight into the hands of extremists. The peace of Jerusalem is, to a measure, in the hands of all the communities which have built its history. So we are going to have to find ways of talking one with another.

One of the consequences of our accepting the sheer complexity of the issue and the profound difficulty we all have in finding any solutions is that we will all be very wary of simplistic analyses of the problem. There are plenty of simple approaches around. They generally begin, 'If it had not been for . . .'. The sentence is completed by the following sorts of statement:

... the growth of the acceptance of Zionist ideology ...

... the Holocaust ...

... Islamic fundamentalism ...

... the PLO use of violence ...

... American Imperialism ...

... the Cold War ...

... the Balfour Declaration ...

Doubtless all these, in different ways, have created or contributed to the unresolved issue of the status of Jerusalem. Any student of history will tell us that before any of these things happened this city was part of a history of conflict and division. Take those ingredients away and others would no doubt have been cast into the pot. Accepting bafflement is part of an honest way forward.

In like manner there must be a resistance to simple solutions – the 'if only . . .' kind of comment.

If only the Israelis had not gone on building settlements around the city . . .

If only Hamas had not blown up those buses in 1996 . . .

If only the Gulf War had not broken out . . .

Doubtless the absence of such events would have changed the story for the better. We cannot, however, escape where we are by denying the realities as they confront us now. That is always hard and drives all parties to accepting the complexity of the issues and so the need for imaginative and fresh thinking.

All of these approaches remind us that the way people construct the realities in their culture is crucial to the possibility of changing things. We are not required to change the facts but we can change our perception of what they mean. This is one of the places where theology and religious perception grow in importance.

Jewish constructs

We can illustrate this by three historical realities. First, Zionism is a philosophy which came to the fore in the late nineteenth century and has been given strength by the terrible events in Jewish history in the twentieth century.[4] The fact of Zionist politics reminds us of something else about the Jewish community. For large parts of their history Jewish people have not given a great deal of thought to the notion of a nation set aside especially for Jewish people. The nation of Israel should not be equated with the essence of Jewish life and culture which thrives across the world in many forms. It also acts as a reminder that not all Jewish people support the Zionist idea or want to live or indeed can live in Israel.

Muslim constructs

Second, the religious significance of Jerusalem for Muslims was enhanced by the Crusades. It became important to establish, in the face of Latin Christian imperialism, that this city had an important place in the history of religion as Muslim people understood it. Christians had no right to exclusive claims! Again, that means that there have been times in Islamic history in which the religious significance of Jerusalem for Muslims has not been very great. Mecca remains the central city for the faith and for pilgrimage.

Christian constructs

Third, not all Christians have seen Jerusalem as critical to the Christian faith. There is an ambivalence in Christian faith about the idea of sacred places. The same ambivalence is experienced in our struggle with the use of the word 'church' – is it a building or a congregation? Is it not the people rather than the place which are set apart for the service of God? It is not surprising, therefore, to find that for large parts of the history of the Church Christians have not been fascinated with the supposedly 'sacred' places. They have been much more concerned for the state of health of the Church – the people of faith – who are in Jerusalem. The 'Jerusalem' above – representing the heavenly vision of peace – is the true meaning of the city in the light of the events of Jesus' life and ministry.

There are, therefore, important parts of Jewish culture and history, Islamic culture and history, and Christian thought and history which attach rather less significance to the place of Jerusalem as religiously important than to the experience of its living communities of faith. More space might be given to the task of agreeing how all its peoples can live together in peace and freedom if all religious traditions put less weight on the place and more on the people.

Most Jews, Muslims and Christians in the world live their faith in the context of their daily living without ever having been to the Holy Land, let alone Jerusalem. Pilgrimage is the luxury of the few, not an essential of faith. The three monotheistic religions have that in common. The faith of Jewish people, of Islamic people and of Christian people is not dependent on what happens to the city of Jerusalem and in the land of Palestine.

This perception further strengthens the wisdom of those who call for Christian pilgrimage to be as much if not more about encounter with the Living Stones – the contemporary Church and people – rather than with the old and dead stones of the history (much of which is open to some dispute!). Pilgrimage which is not about encounter with the living Church can be positively harmful. It romanticises the place and confuses the issue of justice and peace in the contemporary unresolved question of the status of this city. The classic example of this is the approach of the Christian Zionists who have lost the issue of justice in the fog of a misguided understanding of the place of the earthly Jerusalem in the divine economy.

How we see things leads to the social construct we put upon the reality at stake. The New Testament writers are clear that the event of Jesus' ministry, his death in Jerusalem and his resurrection, brought about a radical change of perception about the significance of this city. Jerusalem is the place where Jesus came bringing the hope of the Kingdom. In the mystery of the purpose of God that Kingdom was established through rejection and suffering and death. As a

Jewish person Jesus loved Jerusalem and longed for it. Yet he knew that the experience of rejection would be an end of one order so that the door could open on the new.

In the post resurrection period the focus moved from Jerusalem the place to what the city symbolised of the meaning of the presence of God and of the hope of the future shape of the Kingdom of God. That shift is anticipated in such incidents as the debate Jesus had with the woman at the well in which he said that neither the Samaritan mount nor Jerusalem would be the focus of the worship of the people of God in the future. 'Neither on this mountain nor in Jerusalem...' (John 4:21). It is focused on the interpretation of the teaching of Jesus about the destruction of the Temple and the raising of something new in his resurrection body (Mark 13:1–2 and 14:53–62). The focus of faith moved to the vision of the new Jerusalem – the Jerusalem which is above (Galatians 4:25–6). In the apocalyptic tradition the vision of the new Jerusalem is of the city still to come – the city of peace and beauty where the promise of peace and harmony is fulfilled (Revelation 21).

All of that is understood as the true meaning of the resurrection. Time and again the Gospel writers tell us, 'he is not here, he is risen and gone ahead of his disciples'. The Gospels see the resurrection as opening the door into the mission of the Church. It is not a return to the presence of Jesus in Palestine. The cross is not an unfortunate episode which the resurrection put right so that Jesus could continue his earthly ministry. It is the moment of transformation and the fulfilment of the promise which is for all. It heralds a radical new beginning. The story moves from the city of Jerusalem out into the multiplicity of cities and cultures of the wider world.

That ambivalence, present throughout the Old Testament, about places and buildings as a focus for the meaning of the presence of God among the people is resolved in the risen Christ whose body is the true Temple of God and whose people are to be the hope of the city of peace and justice for all. There must be a deep reticence about identifying the presence of the God who meets us and greets us in the risen

Christ with particular places, however significant they may have been in the story of faith. The God who brought again our Lord Jesus Christ from the dead is not here. That 'not being here' gives the space needed by all who seek to find a new way of living for Jerusalem. The negative 'not on this mountain' is the first key to the positive. Again, it is the absence but not indifference of God which enables growth to happen.

The second step, crucial but difficult to make, is to untie the presence of God from the particularity of our own history. Sectarianism wants God to be for us and so not for them. A discussion which is about proving that God is with one tradition and not the other is sterile and destructive. The God of our brothers and sisters in Islam or Judaism is the one true God whom we Christians have come to experience in Jesus Christ. Critical questions of truth can only be explored with sharpness and integrity when we all resist the temptation to think we have God in our pocket.

If God is not to be seen as particularly present in Jerusalem that must be especially true of any suggestion of a special relationship with any of the faith communities. If we are to use the language of the presence of God we must use it for all or abandon the attempt. That sense of a deep respect for the integrity of the faith of others – a recognition that God is God and cannot be retained within the boundaries of our own convictions – is vital to our witness to the uniqueness of the one true God. God is wholly other than us and yet, we believe, is underneath, surrounding and within all our experience.

There have been and continue to be symbolic moments when that truth has been made visible. The care offered by one faith integrity to another is illustrated, for example, by the historic respect Islam has had for Christianity as expressed in its protection of their places of worship. The Dome of the Rock was almost certainly designed and built by Christians. It has an obvious Byzantine feel to its design. There are many stories of the respect paid by the conquering Muslim leaders in the seventh century to Christian churches and holy places, the exact truthfulness of which is hard to judge. Whatever the exact nature of the truth, the existence of the stories tells of a perception of respect and reticence shown by the new Islamic powers towards the Church.

These stories need telling and integrating in the way the faith communities see each other. They have the potential of taking people nearer to the sacred heart of true religion and enabling a divided society to draw near to the one God.

John Esquito puts it very well:

> Any equitable resolution of the future state of Jerusalem will require all its major religious communities to affirm a pluralistic theology of inclusiveness and religious tolerance in which there are no masters and servants but rather a society in which all citizens recognise their equal status and rights before God as children of Abraham. Therefore, despite important religious differences, all are heirs of a common Judaeo/Christian/Islamic tradition, neighbours and servants of God.[5]

The significance of this comment from Esquito is that it digs down to find important common life and it makes a theological statement leaving the immediate participants to work on the political consequences. We have to think in a theological way which takes us away from the divisive stories – Christians blaming the Jews for the death of Jesus, Jews excluding Palestinian people from the history of the land, Muslims portraying the future as an all-embracing Islamic reality. The stories which remind us that we are all equally children of Abraham are the ones which offer hope of constructing a different and more peace-orientated future. Those are the only ones which have any resonance with the truth of the faith proclaimed by all three traditions.

In the intense heat of the cauldron of conflicts, such as that represented by the unresolved issue of the future of Jerusalem, a lot of things get destroyed. Many of these are things we value. Nevertheless the fire unmercifully destroys all perishables. The vision and hope, however, is that out of such suffering and pain a purer reality of our common life might yet emerge. That gain might offer hope not just to the immediate suffering people of the ancient land we call holy but to the troubled followers of the three monotheistic religions whose origins are with the story of Abraham. The demystifying of the politics of this city might deepen communion and community to peoples who for centuries have gone in different ways on the spiritual journey which Abraham inspired centuries ago. The encounter of Abraham, father of us all, with the King of Salem might yet be a sign of hope for Jerusalem today and all whose faith has been sustained by the events of its extraordinary history.

The European Question

The twentieth century has been one of great turmoil for Europe. The work which has been undertaken in the past fifty years to find some patterns for the unity of Europe illustrates the tensions we face in finding an answer to how we live together across the diversities of our history, culture and faith. These difficulties focus on specific issues.

- Should we have a common monetary policy and currency?
- Should we seek greater and greater political union?
- How far are we to go in integrating different ways of approaching social policy?

These technical issues produce heated debate and often lead people into larger dilemmas.

- Will a common currency undermine national sovereignty?
- Will greater central control lead to disenchantment among the people and so to social disorder?

A century overshadowed by war

As we approach the end of the century we have to take stock of the major shifts in European life which are bound to shape the future and influence the choices we make. For most of the century Europe has been deeply divided. It entered this century under the growing threat of war. The newly united and economically growing Germany became a threat to the rest of Europe. German imperialism challenged British imperialism in the spheres of both industry and of politics. From 1914 to 1945 the continent's politics were overshadowed by two major and devastating world wars. Then for forty years Europe lived under the threat posed by the Cold War and its division between East and West. Huge arsenals of terrifying weapons and large armies faced each other across the heart of the continent. The political life of the wider world was continually drawn into the outcome of this cold hostility between East and West. So war and its threat have dominated European history in this century.

The collapse of the Soviet Empire and the ending of the Cold War has brought Europe a moment of opportunity it has not seen throughout the rest of this century. The dark shadow of war has been lifted from most of its peoples. We approach the twenty-first century with huge opportunities. Failure to address them could have devastating consequences for future generations. We should not underestimate the threat of future division and even conflict.

Under the shadow of the major and appalling conflicts which have dominated the twentieth century other divisions continued to fester. The collapse of the dominant issue of international relations has exposed a number of other conflicts which have been under the surface. In some of the old subservient republics of the former Soviet Union, in Bosnia, in Ireland, and in the Basque country historic unresolved tensions and conflicts are being seen in the clearer light of the post Cold War European community. New more localised nationalisms and historic regional conflicts are coming to the surface. So at a more local level we face the continuing challenge of how we live in mutual respect and peace.

It could be said that we are only just beginning to emerge from the damage done by the First World War. Fed by a jingoistic nationalism on both sides a terrible carnage took place on the fields of Belgium and Northern France. Those who stood out against what was happening were few, treated as traitors and ostracised. The Churches proved themselves ill-equipped to articulate the moral dilemmas of the war and give any sort of a prophetic lead as the carnage went on and on. There was little contact between the Churches in Germany and those in the allied nations. The vast majority of Church leaders seemed to be drawn into the national mood of doing what had to be done to win the war whatever the cost. Like so many other aspects of the old order, the Church came out of that First World War weakened and in decline. It seemed as if the Church and Christendom had failed. It is not surprising that people sought for other sets of ideas to cope with the demands of the twentieth-century world. Religious belief was attacked both philosophically and politically. Logical positivism on the one side and atheistic Marxism on the other undermined the credibility of the faith. Secular socialism began to dominate the politics of dissent.

Far from the First World War being the war to end all wars it ushered in a second conflagration. First there was a period of economic collapse with mass unemployment and large scale poverty. It is easy to forget how deep a wound was left in the consciousness of the peoples of Europe by the want of the 1920s and 30s. The failure to deal with the issues of mass poverty and exclusion contributed to the conditions which led Europe into a second and even bloodier conflict. Europe had failed to resolve the problems of reconstruction after 1918. Europe now had to overcome the terror of the Nazi challenge. If Christendom seemed incapable of helping the peoples of Europe to live at peace, capitalism seemed totally incompetent in the face of the mass poverty experienced in the 20s and 30s. The great optimism of the Industrial Revolution and of the ability of capital to deliver new forms of power gave way to a deep scepticism.

The postwar division of Europe brought to the surface the uselessness of Leninist forms of Marxism to deliver anything better. When, as a result of the war, it became clear how dreadful life was in the Soviet Union and how appalling was the Stalinist terror the hopes of radical communist movements in the West collapsed. We looked at Marxism and said 'no thank you'.

78

The confidence of European people had been undermined in the inheritance of faith and conviction which had endeavoured to shape their history both in the past and the present. The inheritance of both the Church and the Enlightenment looked poor. Neither Christendom nor modernity had served us well.

This loss of confidence encouraged the sort of reductionism which has affected Church and politics in our time. What were the Churches good at in the midst of terrible wars? Answer – the pastoral care of victims. Chaplains and clergy did heroic work in the face of terrible experiences. But the Church was not very good at the macro questions of the morality and the politics of mass war. It seemed to be good mainly with individuals caught up as victims. So the Church has been driven into a pastoral backwater in our culture – good at the pastoral care of individuals and their families but not perceived as having any serious contribution to the meaning of the deeper movements of our history.

Similar distrust can be evidenced against any grand claims for the state or for corporate power in any form. Politics is essentially pragmatic and eclectic – choosing the immediate and practical answer to specific challenges and resisting grand schemes of thought and ideology which threaten to determine what happens. The abuses of the state machinery by both the Nazis and the Stalinists have made people wary of power.

Europe raises larger issues

So not only are the historic institutions and ideologies which formed our culture not trusted today but there is a tendency to make use of them according to their immediate practical effect. The European project, however, has brought back to us important questions about the unity of our culture and has done so in the face of a world which has grown to distrust universal solutions and centralised institutions.

There are complex and paradoxical elements to this. The history of the collapse of Yugoslavia into the contemporary and divided history of Bosnia/Hercegovina illustrates this paradox. In 1945 Tito united the nation and kept a measure of independence for it within the broad orbit of the Soviet dominated Eastern half of Europe. Its internal politics were carefully controlled and designed to hold a balance between the different nationalities who made up this new republic. Unity was achieved by careful control. It seemed to work. The death of Marshal Tito together with the collapse of the Soviet and Communist dominance of Eastern Europe combined to take away the structure which held Yugoslavia together. Efforts at giving political power and fresh identity to the several republics which had formed Yugoslavia collapsed as the different groups and nationalities fought over the land. The dreadful story of war, ethnic cleansing and the tentative efforts at reconstruction are well known and continue. An imposed order had failed. The historic tensions were still there under the surface. Now a bottom up approach ran aground because it seemed impossible to get the different parties to agree. Is it possible to find a solution with consent which does not end up with the outcomes of ethnic cleansing and the three major peoples of the area separated off into ethnically clean political entities? If we throw into the pot the history, where there are perceived 'old scores' to settle – be they of collaboration with the Nazis or of the ancient dominance of the Turks and of Islam – the task of finding some common life which allows people to live for the future in peace becomes doubly difficult. We are cautious about setting up new and imposed structures of unity and we struggle with the task of creating a united way of life within the diverse and sometimes warring factions of Europe. Bosnia is a parable of the struggle Europe has for unity with diversity.

The European project is driven by the experience of the devastation brought to its history by these conflicts. 'Never again . . .' is the sort of sentence which begins the driving force of the argument for a united Europe. The fear of war and a deeper fear of Europe being plunged into a new dark age have driven those whose vision helped to create the

European Union and the Council of Europe. We need structures to help guard our culture and prevent the internal forces
of destruction undermining it. That is the logic of the political
case for the European institutions.

From economics to common culture?

In the postwar years, as the challenge of reconstruction was
faced, economic issues dominated the debate about Europe
and its future. There was a strong desire to avoid the terrible
mistakes of the post 1918 drive for reparation which in the
end broke the fragile democracy in Germany in the 1930s.
We must help one another recover. A free and shared market
was created and with it systems of support for the economy
of European nations who belonged to the Common Market.
The Common Agricultural Policy is an example of agreed
procedures for mutual help to support Europe's large farming
community.

Economic issues still dominate the question of European
unity. The establishment of the European Parliament indicates some movement towards a political restructuring.
Procedures for free borders have led to a greater move in
the direction of political union and cultural interchange. The
dominant issue, nevertheless, remains the shared economy
with finance rather than trade the central issue as we approach
the twenty-first century. The debate about the common currency and with it the need for European banking systems is
at the heart of present European debate. That the Union
is expanding as, first, more Western European nations join
and, second, it moves to include Eastern European nations
formerly in the Soviet Empire should not divert us from the
centrality of the economic issues which dominate Europe at
this time.

The collapse, however, of the Cold War division of Europe
is changing the agenda. Political questions are bound to come
to the surface as countries with very different histories in the
political sphere begin to take their place inside the Union.

81

That will in turn lead to some searching debate about the meaning of Europe. What is it, apart from fear of war and a desire for shared prosperity, which holds us together?

It is from Eastern Europe that some of the deeper questions are being raised. Vaclav Havel, that remarkable President of the Czech Republic and motivater of the movement which brought Czechoslavakian freedom from the Leninist oppression has spoken and written widely on these matters. In a speech delivered in Aachen in May 1996, reported in the *New York Review of Books* (and which I quoted in an article on Europe in *Anvil*), raises just these issues.

> This Europe represents a common destiny, a common complex history, common values, and common culture and way of life. More than that, it is also, in a sense, a region characterised by particular forms of behaviour, a particular quality of will, a particular understanding of responsibility. As a consequence, the borders of this Europe may at times seem fuzzy or variable: it cannot be defined by looking at a school atlas or studying a list of members of the European Union or of the countries that could join if they wish, such as Norway, Switzerland, or Iceland. This is why any discussion of this ... Europe is more difficult, and occurs less often. Yet this is precisely where all debates about Europe and its future should begin.[1]

In other writings Havel has made it clear that he views the technical questions of trade and the economy and borders as a long way secondary to this the central issue – in what lies the common life of Europe? What shared understanding should undergird its technical arrangements for its common life? That is a cultural question and, for Christians, a theological one. In Europe it is also a question about the nature of the Church.

The changing role of the Church

The Christian community is going to have to share in this debate on the same terms as everyone else. That includes an acceptance of the profound changes which have happened to us in the twentieth century. We cannot go back. We can, however, recognise the shift that is required of us. The picture of the Archbishop of Paris making public apology in 1997, on behalf of the French Catholic Church, for its collusion with the Nazis in the deportation and destruction of the Jews of France during the wartime years of occupation is a powerful symbol of what is at stake. The spiritual and theological resources of the Church were not up to the challenge of Fascism. A desire to continue to share influence with power confused the leadership of the Church (as it did many others). That desire is symbolic witness of the failure of Christendom to deliver moral and spiritual protection to the people. Christendom was too much bound up with the Church's participation in power and in trying to ensure cultural conformity. If the Archbishop of Paris' action has any substance to it it must mean a farewell by the Church to any desire to return to such a role and place in the community. The regeneration of the Church must happen when its power – its capacity to influence events and people – arises out of its service. That is the real meaning of its worship.

The Church too has a journey to make if it is to experience and offer something of the meaning of freedom in love. Clearly the sort of status held by the Church which led to its failure to protect the weak and abused is a status which emasculates the heart of the meaning of the Church. That experience in France exactly parallels the incapacity of the established Church in England, and of the rest of the Churches who defined themselves in relation to the established Church, to give any clear prophetic lead in the face of the brutal ungodly nationalism which fuelled the destruction of the trenches in 1914–18.[2] Both the form and the substance of Christendom failed the demands of the Kingdom of God at a critical moment in the forming of our modern world.

So we enter this discussion by resolutely leaving the past, accepting our responsibility for its failure and by a process of renewal which looks to serve and enable rather than control and direct. Like all reformations of the Church a great deal of clutter will have to go. Especially those aspects of our order which leave the impression on our culture of bodies still stuck with hierarchical and non-inclusive systems of organisation. The continuity is in the vision of God and our shared responsibility for the journey of faith with all who have gone before us.

The unity of the European Churches

This helps clear the ground for us to consider what we need to tackle as part of a process of the reformation of our culture in Europe to offer peaceful and good space for the journey which is ahead. A penitential and careful approach by the historic Churches enables them to face up to the contribution Christianity has made to the division of Europe by its own divisions. Elsewhere in this book we note the way the historic divide between Western and Eastern Churches has affected the history of Palestine and of Jerusalem in particular. The divisions of the sixteenth and seventeenth centuries have fed the conflicts of Europe and debilitated the capacity of the Church to be a focus for peace across the diversity of our cultures. Christians, it seems, find it hard to live in communion with each other. Yet, deep in the history of the development of European culture, is the story of the gospel. Important and enduring goods have been brought to Europe through the work of the Churches. What they stand for is, in an important way, critical to a sense of the unity of Europe.

The ecclesiological and ecumenical issues are crucial to the way the Church serves the emerging future of European life. The endeavours of those who have sought to open real lines of communication across the divisions of the Churches bear witness to the central importance of the Christian community recovering its sense of communion. In the end, as with the European question itself, this is not a technical issue about order but one about shared vision and a sense of the importance of making the journey together in pursuit of the vision. Unity is in the unity of God and the consistency of the heavenly vision of the meaning of love at the heart of all being – the love which works for the freedom of all creation. The goods that have come to Europe from its Christian inheritance are in part consequences of the Church catching this vision. Technical questions are important and cannot be evaded but they are secondary to a sense of belonging together which comes from a shared experience and conviction about the vision.[3]

Neither sectarian nor centralist

There is a parallelism between the political agenda and the ecclesiastical one. Both have to resist sectarianism and centralisation at one and the same time if a sense of common life which respects and even nurtures diversity is to be encouraged. Sectarianism goes down the road of isolated individualism – the excluding of those who do not meet the requirements of the group. In political terms sectarianism undermines democracy. The essence of democratic politics is that all are represented. Government happens by the outcomes of the way the whole community negotiates its business through its representatives. The essence of Church, as opposed to sect, is that all sorts and conditions of human life can find shelter within its communion – the free grace of God to a broken world makes for an open and inclusive Church.

Centralisation, by contrast, travels the road of imposed order. The definition of citizenship is in a willingness to conform to the given order. There is little sense of the mobility of social life and of the need for authority to respond continually to and assist the changing patterns of people's lives. In like manner conformity to a centralised and given order cannot be taken as an adequate understanding for the Church. The Church too has not finished its journey – there are still new experiences and understandings to be encountered. Communion must not be allowed to collapse into an imposed conformity. The whole experience of the twentieth century militates against it. Communion implies a real sense of consent.

The hopefulness in all of this is that in their heart convictions all the Churches of Europe have principles and theologies which resist both the autonomy of the isolated group and the unrestricted power of centralised authority. We may have very different histories but there are common lines of thinking – which ought not to surprise us when we all study the same Scriptures and seek vision and hope from the same Lord. For some the predominant concern will be how they hold back the forces of autonomy and sectarianism; for others how they balance a strong given order with the liberty of the Spirit. From the independent Baptist churches through to the Vatican we have all got to have the courage to recognise a shared life in the gospel message. We are neighbours and share together the historic inheritance of the Christian hope. It is ours only because it is theirs as well.

So the endeavour by the Churches at rediscovering a form of unity which enjoys and accepts diversity runs alongside the political search for a shared life in Europe which brings common values to the surface and so enables communion across the range of our culture.

Shared values?

Havel believes that we share a common inheritance of culture and values and that this is the essential definition of what makes Europe. Europe is now established as a multi-cultural and multi-faith community. Many of its people reject religious faith and live by values which they do not relate to any spiritual foundation. This is the world we are living in. We have already rejected any notion of going back. We must now look at how we make this emerging world something good and positive.

The good things which come, for Christians, out of the inheritance of faith which others can own from their personal perspective are many. The interplay of Europe's Christian inheritance with its Enlightenment culture in the context of a postmodern and diverse world might be productive of a great deal of value. Havel could be right – we have more in common than sometimes we admit.

Shared values for the individual in society

One of the secrets of a healthy community is the capacity it demonstrates for providing space for individuals to flourish and for society to grow and develop in goodness. We do not have to choose between the individual and the community. At the heart of the Christian vision of God is an understanding of being in which love is always a communion of persons in freedom. The unity of God is seen in the Trinity of Persons. That vision of God has encouraged Christians to search for community which both welcomes and nurtures each person for their own sake and which builds a common life as a result. We persist with the struggle to make something of this real in the present because of the driving power of the vision. The history of the creation of the many different forms of church might be seen in this light. From the search for the purity of the monastic community or the Anabaptist fellowship to the struggle to integrate a diverse and troubled humanity into an inclusive and open form of congregational life in the heart of divided neighbourhoods, the same vision inspires the community building/person affirming work.

Out of that might come four dualities of value which begin to define our inheritance.

Freedom and responsibility

Freedom working to enable individuals and communities to accept and deploy responsibility for their own lives is at the heart of the meaning of European democracy. That is rooted in a conviction about the unique integrity and worth of every person's life irrespective of status, origin or personal identity. What holds us together is sharing a common human identity – not being the same.

The success of such freedom is dependent upon an acceptance of its responsibility. The assumption of our culture is that people and communities are meant to be adult and make the choices about their own lives for themselves. That is why the law should protect the integrity of the individual and democracy, the duty of the whole community to act by consent.

Of course we are always having to work on the conflicts this creates. Balancing the right of individuals to privacy in order to protect their right to determine their own lives with the importance of an open commitment to truth in the community is not easy. The practical outcomes by which we choose to resolve these dilemmas have to survive the test of freedom working for responsibility. To wave the flag of freedom without recognising its essential bond with responsibility might endanger freedom itself. Responsibility cannot be properly accepted under constraint. Freedom is its very basis. In tackling issues such as the liberty of the media over and against the rights of the individual citizen the answer chosen – be it media self-regulation or a law protecting privacy – has to meet the value criteria of freedom working for responsibility if it is both to protect the person and build an open and truthful community.

Justice and duty

Although the legal systems of Europe vary and have different traditions there are common roots of value. Justice has many sides to it. It is about the impartial and equal treatment of all citizens by the law. It is the protection of individuals and communities from the abuses of power. It seeks to determine the outcome of conflicts between individuals and the community with fairness and independence. It punishes the guilty without yielding to any passion for revenge and it apportions responsibility and determines outcomes in all civil disputes.

The concept of justice arising out of Christian faith is rooted in the righteousness of God – the consistent way in which God acts upon the world and for people. The vision of God brings to the surface the equal dignity and worth of all in the light of the persistent love of God for all irrespective of life experience. God's justice seeks to bring people back into full participation in the community through the power of forgiveness. The doing of justice leads to liberty and to community.

Justice is dependent upon a sense of relationship. The love of God redeems and restores broken relationships. That redemptive experience creates a bond of relationship which is transforming. A new way of living emerges from the redemptive act of God. That is mirrored in the essential bond between justice and duty in the community. The obligations of citizenship in civic society parallel the obligations of neighbourly love in the spiritual realm. Justice cannot operate if people do not accept any sense of duty to the community in which the law is at work. That is why, in the absence of justice in oppressive societies, people do not accept a duty to the law. If a just framework of social order flourishes when citizens accept their duty to live by it, a flourishing community of mutual obligation is dependent upon a commitment to justice undergirding the social order.

In European culture this balance has been expressed in the sovereignty and independence of the courts to whom is entrusted even the controlling of governments when they threaten the people with injustice.

Peace and respect

The priceless gift of peace is fundamental to a society which provides the freedom for all its people to pursue their several vocations. It is one of the deepest experiences of worship to find contentment, a need to right wrongs with one's neighbours and to live for peace in the world. Christians, caught by the vision of God, are peacemakers. That is because God is essentially a God of Peace – from the heart of whose being flows the love which is prepared for the costly action to overcome conflict by the removal of its causes. The vision of the future in the Christian tradition is focused on the heavenly Jerusalem (city of Peace) and the creative harmony of creation at peace with the Creator and with itself.

Peaceful communities live by respecting others. That respect recognises a duty to provide space for people to live their lives as they choose. Imposed beliefs and oppressive systems of order destroy peace in the community. The Christians who show respect to their Islamic brothers and sisters by helping protect their freedom to worship and to bring up their children by their own faith are witnessing to an essential truth rooted in their own experience of God. Religious imperialism, which has helped fuel wars across our history, has to give way to mutual respect rooted in a desire to live with our neighbours in peace. It is interesting to hear Father Elias Chacour in the Holy Land, where he has worked tirelessly for peace with justice for the Palestinian people, talk about times when he has encouraged the local Muslims to use the church when they were without a mosque. The desire for peace in one setting often leads to its practice in another.

It is a commitment to peace expressed through mutual respect which undergirds the European tradition of tolerance in the modern world. Not only is it critical to the flourishing of our multi-faceted society it is rooted in both the spiritual inheritance of the gospel and the Enlightenment understanding of reason.

Truth and integrity

An open society values and lives by the truth, however painful. Secrecy belongs to a world of fear. The underworld of the secret services, of spying and counter-espionage belongs to a world where there is war or the threat of war and where peoples cannot trust one another. We keep secrets when there is fear and lack of trust. At all levels of the flourishing of individuals, families and communities, truth openly accepted makes for growth, secrets hold nothing but danger. We know the damage done in families when the truth is withheld from its members.

A commitment to open truth is integral to the Christian faith. Its heart assertion is that, in Jesus Christ, God made open to the world the secret of the truth from all eternity. God opens up the heart of the being of love to the world. The Christian revelation is an open secret. The Christian understanding of God is of One who reveals truth and who does not hide from the world what it needs both to see and know for its life and movement towards its true destiny.

That truth is shared in ways which underline the integrity of people. The Christian truth came to the world in a human being – face to face with us. There is no question of imposition or manipulation. The Church may be tempted to travel those roads but the gospel offers it no comfort if it does. The truth is open, offered in freedom and respects the integrity of those to whom it is addressed. The fact of the incarnation tells only this story. No other can be made to fit what God has done.

These values are expressed in many ways. The commitment to freedom of information is an example of the principle at work. Information about individuals cannot be held in secret without the person concerned knowing what is there. So there is protection of their integrity both by the protection of that information from general public access (confidentiality) and by ensuring that individuals have control of the information which concerns their own life in the community. Secrecy is out, confidentiality is in.

These four boundaries mark out our culture. They draw on our inheritance and shape themselves for the needs of a diverse and changing world. They should inform the renewal of the Church as it seeks a deeper unity and the emerging forms of our common life in Europe. The twenty-first century could yet offer to Europe a new flourishing of its life and a new and creative contribution to the wider world and to the survival of our planet.

The exposition of these themes by the Christian community and the determination of the Church to seek to live by them in unity and mutual love is the essential way in which the Church will make a contribution to the reshaping of Europe and its culture for a safer and freer future.

Ireland – the Pre-Modern Moving to the Postmodern World

An almost total lack of comprehension and an overriding sense of bafflement inhabit the minds of those who try and understand the Irish question from outside of Ireland. The British find it all especially confusing. Sometimes the encounter with Irish politics seems like a journey back through history to an age that has long gone for everyone else. It seems as though Ireland is struggling to make sense of a postmodern world without having fully come to terms with modernism. It is paradoxical. Large numbers of people both belong to and attend the Christian Church in the North as well as the South of Ireland and yet find it a deep struggle to live at peace with their neighbours. The strange sight of people in uniforms marching out of church and straight through hostile neighbourhoods seems to be a contradiction. How can people worship God one minute and the next provoke their neighbours by marching through communities which are not willing to welcome them? Yet they are not alone in the world in behaving as if the end of religious and cultural identity justifies the means of asserting it.

There lies the issue – what is right? We have a right to march. We have a right to the land. We have a right, and we will impose it by whatever means are available to us. There is no agreement, in Ireland, on who is entitled to what. It is the classic example of the critical importance of the story believed determining the shape of understanding of the issues.[1]

Story number one. This is the story of the centuries of English and British oppression of the Irish people. The struggle to free the Irish people from this colonialism cannot be complete until the North of Ireland is united again to the rest of the country. The Irish people are not yet wholly free and will not be until the colonial British are out of the island and Ireland is united again. The strength of the story lies in its grasp of some of the truth.

Story number two. This is the story of the Catholic oppression of the people of Ireland and the brave struggle of the minority Protestant community to hold the door of liberty open in Ireland. The pope must have no jurisdiction over this land and its people. The Irish state, set up in Dublin, is a Catholic state and the unity of Ireland on its terms will mean the death of the Protestant cause. Again, the story has some plausibility and contains some of the truth of the story.

The power of these stories in the imagination of the people has been deepened through struggle, wars, heroism, cultic song and ritual. It is kept alive by political and ecclesiastical division. Nationalism reads the story one way, Unionism the other.[2]

Story number three involves the British. Across the water these conflicting stories have been fuelled by the at best ambivalent and at worst destructive contribution made by successive generations of English and British interference. The Irish question, as it was called, divided British politics in the latter half of the nineteenth century and threatened to undo the structure of the establishment. Ireland became a battleground between two conflicting views of British consti- tutional ideas.[3] Ironically, the liberal cause for disestablishment in the nineteenth and early twentieth cen- turies was supported by both dissenters and Roman Catholics. Together they resisted the Protestant establishment of the Church of England.[4] Ireland became a symbol of this cause. So we have Unionism and Nationalism and the British involvement.[5]

The persistent pressure of such a complex set of stories is to insist that you have to make up your mind on which side you stand. Part of the deadly mix is the insistence that you have to take sides and belong to one story or another. In taking sides it becomes impossible to hear the truth in the story of the other side. There seems to be little ground between for movement. Driving across the North of Ireland early one July I was very struck by the way the road took us through the villages and small towns representing the historic division of the Northern Irish community. In village number one the roads were bedecked with British flags in preparation for the great celebration of July 12 when the victory of William of Orange would be celebrated on the streets with carnival, processions and bonfires. In village number two not a flag in sight. July 12 represents the history of repression. So the journey went on from Protestant to Catholic village. A small corner of Ireland divided between two peoples and two understandings of history. The public image is one of a divided society with little ground for movement between.

The stories told to the generations, to hold the culture firm to this history, seek to provide answers to the questions – whose land is this? Can it ever be free of the tyranny of the abuse of power? This has been a struggle for political and economic control of the land and its resources. Ireland has been a land of conquest and rebellion. Its story has been fatally drawn into the historic struggles for power in England and not least the seventeenth-century struggle between the Catholic Stuart cause and the Protestant Orange cause. It is ironic that a fundamentally English struggle for power, long since buried in the mists of British history, has had such a persistently damaging effect upon Ireland. Something of a deep English guilt may be one of the driving forces behind the desire to find a solution to the 'Irish Problem'. It is as much an English problem as an Irish one. So there are three interlocking stories – the English, Nationalist and Unionist stories. It is not surprising that they are still locked together struggling to find a way of telling the story which liberates all parties for a different and more peaceful future.

Facing the religious element

We cannot escape the fatal religious ingredient in all of this. In vain do we say that the basis of the story is really about politics and culture, thus trying to extricate religion from any serious responsibility in all of this. Sadly, the words 'Protestant' and 'Catholic' have real substance in the story. The fire is fuelled by the history and the perceptions about Christian faith: the pope as anti-Christ (not so long ago believed by large numbers of English people as well), the Protestants as heretics and oppressors (fed by the sectarian attitudes of the nineteenth-century papacy); the Irish state as a plot to impose Catholicism on an unwilling Protestant population. It is a story which the Irish constitution, let alone the behaviour of the Catholic Church in Ireland, has done little to dispel in the early years of the Republic.

Religion becomes a powerful force to give an eternal and unchallengeable dimension to the politics. God is on your side. That brings the argument to an end. When there is nothing left to talk about except to preach across the divide what is left but battle and trouble? So we talk about 'the Troubles'. Religion is part of that trouble. This is the negative way of saying it has to be part of the solution. To start with the negative is to tell the story that has to be left behind. A story which uses religion to justify sectarianism is corrupt. Religion which allows itself so to be used is corrupt. One of the stories which will need to be told when a solution has been agreed is of those in the Churches who quietly but effectively resisted sectarianism.

Lest the British dump all the problem on the Irish side of the water we need to accept that on the British side of the Irish Sea the community has not come to terms with its own history and the effect of it on others. We cannot evade the perception that the persistent involvement of Britain in the six counties in the North is the last vestige of British colonialism in Ireland. For centuries the English have attempted to suppress the Irish by force. They have never succeeded. Simply forgetting the past will not do. We cannot make deep progress in restoring the divisions and abuses of power in our past, and overcoming the way religious truth and institutions have served these causes, by hoping everyone will forget the story. The story is alive and well in Ireland. If it is alive there we cannot bury our heads and hope it will just go away. The hidden sense of responsibility and even guilt needs addressing and clearing. Burying the English theological divide will not help. The difficult story of the religious struggle in England and Scotland has been carried into Ireland. This matter embraces both the attitudes and policies adopted towards Catholicism in England and the unresolved agendas of the established Church in relation to the rest of Protestantism in England. The growing recognition that we are living at a moment of profound shift in our culture and our constitution might just provide the opportunity needed in England to move away from some buried but not dead stories of religious sectarianism and intolerance. Then we might begin to play a creative role in working alongside the rest of the participants in this tragic story.

Getting the story right

Every story told to sustain a sectarian history has the effect of binding people and cultures. The true story liberates. The false or partial one binds. This realisation might provide a way which opens the story up. Let us exorcise the false stories. Falsity is not only to be found in the partiality of the story and its divisive effect. It is to be found in the discovery that it is untrue at all sorts of levels. What truth there is will only shine in another framework of understanding.

One of the paradoxes of a situation like the Irish one is that people's lives are not lived simply within the bounds of these stories. The struggle to break free is evidenced every-where. The sense of delight and hopefulness when the first ceasefire was announced and the peace process started is evidence that deep in the communities is another and more

wholesome story. The subtlety and interchange of relationships between the different communities has been placed
under great strain by the powerful impact of the troubles but
by no means destroyed. The human spirit cannot be so easily
crushed by the false sectarian stories of the old culture. In
what other place in the world have Church leaders worked
so hard together to help people ride above the forces of
sectarianism? Do not wives and mothers, brothers and sisters
of those who have died through the violence suffer and feel
in the same way irrespective of where they come from? Much
good work continues to be done to enable these communities
of suffering to find peace together.

Once again, it becomes important to look for the story
which offers liberation and hope. Nationalist, Unionist,
British, Catholic and Protestant can all find ways of telling
the story that way. Without denying the power of the corrupt
stories told of this situation we must not yield to them. There
are other ways of seeing and understanding the experience
of our Irish brothers and sisters. It is to that possibility that
we must turn our attention.

The theological task

The uncoupling of the divine story from the sectarian story
is a good place to begin. If our faith in God rooted in what
we have seen in the work of Jesus Christ is inclusive and
liberating in its effect, then the sphere of politics is one of
the fields of human life in which we must give this real shape.
The close involvement of religion in the Irish question drives
us to look again at theological themes.

The public and powerful presence of the Church – both
Catholic and Protestant – and the rhetoric associated with
religion in Ireland (from the pulpit to the graffiti on the street
walls) might point us to think again about the nature of God's
presence and of God's Word in our history and experience.
The easy association of God with the causes we espouse might
lead us to think again. Is God to be found with such ease and

certainty? Does God speak with such immediate clarity calling people to rally to the flag?

The God who is not readily present and who is not so free with words might be the God who opens the way to freedom. The God who is not here and who holds to silence in the face of our noise may be the God of truth who sets us free. The God who is not where we are leads us on to new experience and to inhabit new worlds. He is not here. The resurrection tells a story of one who is ahead of us drawing us on into a new journey of faith and discovery. The gods, therefore, who lead the marches and justify the violence and the struggle, become empty idols whose only power is in the minds of those who are captured by them. There is no pillar of fire heading the march down the street and no hidden army of heaven sustaining the armed struggle. Those who go those ways go alone. We must speak with clarity about the distance of the true God from such divisive and destructive behaviour.

Similarly the babel of voices clamouring to justify the partial visions of different sections of the community draws no word from God. Heaven is silent in the face of such noise. The God who speaks is the God who has spoken with such decisive effect in the word and work of Jesus Christ. What more needs to be said? The noise will have to die before the Word of God is heard in the silence. The Word which speaks in the silence and the presence which calls us on from the future is the one we have heard in Jesus Christ. It is relatively easy to delude ourselves into allying the Church to a particular cause. It is much harder to try and justify our cause as the cause of Jesus Christ. It just will not work.

The absence of God and the silence of God are not indicators of the lack of love. Such truths lead not to agnosticism and atheism but to a new faith. Our response to this discovery is a challenge to move. If God is not here then we must travel. If God is not speaking we must learn to be silent and listen. By not being here and by not speaking we are given space in the divine economy for new thought and action – for understanding the story in a different and more inclusive way.

The Irish question challenges not just Irish Christians but all Christians to think afresh about God. There can be no hope and no future in any sectarian understanding of divinity. It is not surprising, therefore, to find that Ireland is a context in which fresh thinking is always happening about the shape and content of the theological task.

The God whom we encounter in Jesus Christ gives the world freedom to change and grow. That must be rooted in the actual realities of our lives in the community. This is not some vapour which threatens to evaporate in the face of the heat of human struggle. It is a persistent challenge and opportunity to seek the new way. How might that be in a circumstance like that of Ireland? We must be careful not to impose solutions. The task is to help people who do carry the responsibility to find the space which truth offers to them to travel the way of love in freedom for themselves. Solutions are the last thing needed in Ireland. There is a superabundance already. It is the process of listening and of discovery which leads to something new.

Theology seeking good stories

The journey might take people down a number of possible roads. The first might be one which searches the history for different and more common stories. History is of particular importance in the Irish context. The telling of stories is a powerful part of the culture. So finding the right and the liberating stories is a critical route into the theological task. It is vital to education and the opening of new insights for the future.

Some parts of the story, which have been partly forgotten or whose significance has not been fully recognised, bring divided communities together. The imaginative story of the encounter of the gospel between Ireland and Scotland, Wales and England is a story full of good things. We can have the courage to go back behind the history of struggle. The recovery of an interest in Celtic spirituality and thought brings people together across the divides. Unionist, Catholic, British – Catholic and Protestant communities find refreshment in this part of our common history. The communities of reconciliation both Protestant and Catholic are sustained by such history. From Iona and Corrymeela on the one side to the creative work of the modern Catholic orders the love of that free and unifying spirituality of the early Celtic saints brings broken worlds together.

St Patrick, in particular, is a person whose formative witness in Ireland is attractive to all. He belongs to an era before the divisions and the troubles and so cannot be enclosed within the sectarian tragedy of more recent times. We have to come to him by leaving the constraints of our Protestant and Catholic history and of the divide of the North and the South. Possessed by none he becomes a person for all – one in whom people can come together. All are in his debt. Patrick is before Catholic and Protestant. All may draw strength from his story.

Seeing both Patrick and the Celtic saints in this way ought to inspire the production of educational material and studies in these matters which command confidence in all communities. Children in Catholic and public schools might yet study from the same scripts and begin to form a mind which brings them together for the future. How history and the history of the Church are taught in Ireland might yet be a fruitful area for common reflection and the adoption of new ways of learning and so of seeing. Giving the children and young people of Ireland the opportunity to tell the story anew is one way of opening up a new future for all.

The inescapable problem of the Church

Other parts of the history can cross the deepest of divides. It is interesting to note how Protestants in the North call Roman Catholic churches 'chapels'. Who are the nonconformists and dissenters? We may well find that aspect of Protestant nonconformist history and Catholic history can speak of not too dissimilar journeys in relation to the establishment. The history of the struggle to have the Church of Ireland disestablished, which symbolised a commitment to end the English domination of the political, social and economic life of Ireland, might draw together all communities who were excluded by such constitutional provision. Irish Anglicans have no desire to go back on this act of liberation. Protestants and Catholics might tell their stories to one another and find some common themes.

It is often as we dig into the meaning of suffering that we discover a shared story with those whom we thought to be our enemy. In telling the story of working communities in Ireland would not Catholic and Protestant communities be talking similar language? It is a strange irony that working-class communities, so deeply divided in the North of Ireland, look so similar. Poverty, fear of unemployment, bewilderment at economic change, the struggles of family life in streets of back to back houses, domestic violence and the difficulties faced by women in these communities, the drift of young people away to other parts of the world to escape the greyness of such living – are not these matters of common interest to all who have suffered them? It is only the graffiti which distinguishes their cultural origins. Large families brought up in the back streets of working-class Protestant Belfast might tell rather similar stories to those in working-class Catholic communities. Who will bring these stories together that they may hear each other? Would not the themes of solidarity, violence, the struggle against poverty, the desire to escape and form a new life elsewhere be common?

There is, therefore, a historical task of looking in new ways at what people have experienced and finding roads which link communities together. These roads need clearing of the weeds and clutter and the barriers which prevent people exploring them. And there is the theological task of talking in ways about God which undo the sectarian abuse of religion. Those who have worked hard to move along such roads need support and encouragement from the Churches.

There is a third road to explore. That is how the Churches struggle against the powerful sectarian ecclesiologies within their own beings. It would be easy for the issue of sectarianism to be externalised. A sect becomes a small denomination with a narrowly defined understanding of the faith. It will usually be fundamentalist or apocalyptic in attitude. So sectarianism has nothing to do with the historic mainstream Churches. By definition the Catholic, Anglican, Presbyterian and Methodist Churches cannot be sectarian. Supposing sectarianism is a state of mind – a construct of the world which excludes those outside? If that is the case it has little to do with the structure of the particular denomination. Roman Catholics and mainstream Protestants could be deeply sectarian under such a definition – demanding conformity and excluding those who refuse. By contrast tiny groups of Christians meeting apart from these formal historic institutions can be catholic and inclusive.

The meaning of the Church in response to the way we experience the gospel has to be thought through in all the settings of our contemporary life. The question is not, therefore, an exclusively Irish question. As we will see in other contexts none of us can escape the force of the question. What is the meaning of the Church in our own history and culture? The Irish experience has raised to the surface the issue of the nature of catholicity and of its relationship to the formal orders of the Church. Those who wrestle with these matters in the sharp setting of Ireland may have vital things to teach the whole Church as it struggles with the meaning of Church in a pluralistic age.

One of the things we are all going to have to acknowledge is the incompleteness of the Church as we know and experience it. The New Testament struggle to form the new Christian community across the historic divisions of both religion and culture in the Jewish and the Greek worlds is not over. One of the marks of the Church is its persistent battle within its own soul for the gospel story of welcome to all and against the sectarian temptations which can even present themselves in the guise of orthodox faith.

The Church is incomplete. It is especially so when it has formed itself in divisive ways. The Catholic Church cannot be catholic whilst many Christians are outside its community. The Protestant Church cannot be apostolic when it is cut off from communities to whom the apostles were sent to proclaim the liberating truth of the risen Christ. No Church can claim to be holy and one when it is not in fellowship with those called apart by God in Christ to bear witness to the hope offered to the world in Jesus. Churches become sectarian in their life when they fail to accept their incompleteness and that part of their essential life is outside their formal structures.

The avoidance of the alluring temptation of sectarianism, with the easy certainty it gives, begins with a clear acceptance of the disjunction between the Church as we know it and the vision of love in freedom offered to the world in Jesus Christ. There is a profound danger in the thesis that you can only have the gospel if you have the Church. In our modern world there is a way of saying that which is problematic and a hindrance to the task that needs to be faced by the Church. The form of the Church is under constant judgement in the context of its life. It shares in the common human difficulty of responding to the vision. Saying that involvement in the good news of Jesus Christ means involvement with the community Christ forms is not the same as saying the Church is part of the package we have to accept when we are drawn by the gospel hope of love in freedom at the heart of God's being.

The help the Church brings to the task is not the bringing of an imposed solution but a sharing in the journey and a willingness to assist in giving it direction. It does this not from certainty but from vulnerability. Its own confession of its incompleteness opens the way for the whole community to face up to the change needed if sectarianism is to be overcome. We need each other and the Church can offer direction by a humble acceptance that this truth begins within its own communion. We each suffer a wound which only those from whom we are separated can heal. Our life and health is, to a measure, in the hands of others and especially those who are on the other side.

So the question becomes not what we can offer to others but what are we ready to receive from them? The interdependent reality of love and grace leads first to learning to receive if we are to be set free to give. That surely is the meaning of the foot-washing story in John 13. Only when our feet have been washed can we find the strength to take the towel and minister to others. Anything less is charity and creates old dependencies not new communities. We are in the business, if the gospel has truth in it, of creating new community.

A sense of Church in which we know part of our life is elsewhere, and we must recover relationship to it, requires time, patience and an open willingness to listen and to learn. The Church is called to open up lines of conversation. Conversation as part of listening and learning is important. Good doctrines of the Church will be on the search for those places where such conversation is taking place. The good news is that it is happening. At all levels, from the public level of leadership through to informal bonds of community across the church denominational barriers, Church is being formed and reformed.[6] The formal life of the Church can either promote and support such conversation or deny it and find it a threat to its own sense of security. Safe and supported places of conversation help create new climates of culture and so new opportunities for communities to break down the walls of hostility and find freedom in love together.

It is always hard work. Whether that hard work involves taking the lid off the difficult issues of denominational education, or of the realities of domestic life where families bridge the divide. Mixed marriages and the upbringing of children are the sort of practical issues which the conversations will be about. Does the Church see the realities of communities sharing together even in the heart of their own home life as problem or possibility? The answer to that sort of question reveals whether the Church has understood the temptation of sectarianism or not.

The interplay between the work done in the wider political and social community and that done in the Churches is crucial. In an issue as complex and longstanding as this, different chapters of the story of its resolution will have different parties in the lead role. Sometimes the politicians can move the story on, sometimes the Churches, sometimes the wider leadership in the whole community, sometimes grass roots sensibilities, sometimes the artistic prophets. In a postmodern world where diversity and flexibility are the hallmarks of the emerging culture we must be open for many different ways in which the story might be told. That is why none, not even the Church, should try and predict how the journey will unfold. The conviction rooted in the story of resurrection that the future belongs to those who build across the divisions of our humanity is the inner driving power to make for change.

These explorations mean that our brothers and sisters in Ireland will have much to contribute to the shaping of the future. In the mystery of the divine life it is from the heart of conflict and struggle that new truth can emerge. It will come, not from those who are committed to keep the battle going, but from those who listen, who wait and who work through the hardship to the future yet to be fully revealed. Those who have encountered the story of Ireland today and the depth of the faith of its peoples know of the potential riches of understanding for the benefit of all.

Section III

Community, Communion and Living Well with Diversity

It is possible that our human dream of community is but a dream and has no hope of reality. The gritty business of daily life functions better by notions of enlightened or not so enlightened self-interest.

If the sense of the divine is not a whim without meaning then the hope of community is not just a dream which passes with the coming of the dawn. If there is truth at stake in this we must attend to the way we construct our culture which includes the many faces of human experience. The twentieth century has brought to an end all stories which come with the ultimate solution to the building of human community. Those idealistic nightmares have caused death and disaster across our own age.

Community has to be built with what there is on the foundation of visions which are open to all. The neat and tidy edifices constructed by those pursuing the destructive 'isms' of the twentieth century must give way, in our culture, to the many different structures created out of the networks and cultures of the highways and byways.

The conviction that 'nothing will be the same' provides the context rather than the barrier to building community today. The encouragement is that many have reached the end of that isolated selfish individualism which is one way of shaping a postmodern world. The vision of love driving the energy of our desire for community – for shared enterprise across the diversity of our life – is the hope which opens the door to something good.

8

The Meaning of Community

Nowhere has the uncertainty of our postmodern world hit us so hard as in the field of the trust between politicians and people. The flight from the universal and the modern has gone hand in hand with growing cynicism about all power-based institutions which affect and govern our lives. Whether it is Brussels or Westminster, the Benefits Office or the Local Authority, the School Governors or the Housing Office, the Crown or the Church – there can be little doubt that trust and confidence have, in different ways, run away from these sorts of bodies. They are perceived as belonging to the past, perpetuating cultures of the past and ill-equipped to serve the values and needs of an emerging flexible and multi-faceted social order.[1]

Concern about the accountability of power and about its capacity to deceive both the people and even its own self is not new. Some of the most important work on the nature of power and the meaning of our life in relation to it has been done in our own century. A return, for example, to that devastating critique of power relations of Reinhold Niebuhr, *Moral Man and Immoral Society* (1932)[2] rooted in his own pastoral and preaching ministry in Detroit, would serve to remind us of the long history of dis-ease with corporate power. Niebuhr's work is classic and prophetic. It is rooted, however, in certain convictions about the reality of social experience and about human nature. His views arose from a deeply held and reasoned faith in God. Niebuhr was sceptical about the capacity of the individual. Some have suggested that his view of humanity is too gloomy and lacks the confidence of a sense of the wonder and goodness of God's creation.

However, it is difficult to lay stress on human possibility in the face of the manipulative and abusive use of power as he witnessed it in the American corporate sector in the years of the Depression. Corporate delusion and even evil seemed to be much more pertinent. Questions of justice seemed to be more pertinent than ones concerning compassion and charity. His work, however, leads not to despair but to a realistic analysis which provides the framework for a corporate response in the name of justice. It did give people hope. The emphasis on justice gave people confidence that it was possible to find a human and principled response to the corporate challenges of the mid-twentieth century.

Niebuhr believed that, in the modern world, democratic institutions offered the right framework for accountability for all corporate power. They provided the best hope for justice and for the containment of the corporate nature of twentieth-century social and economic power.

In the face of the post 1945 East/West divide Niebuhr set about justifying democracy as the only way we knew which could offer people protection against power abuse.[3] He was responding to the postwar division of the world and of the struggle between the two great systems of the second half of the twentieth century – Communism evidenced in the Soviet Union and its Empire and shaped by Leninism and Stalinism, and Western Democracy with its commitment to individual freedom and to capitalist liberal economies.

It is sometimes thought that *Children of Light and Children of Darkness* marks a retreat from the radicalism of his earlier writings. Certainly the days when he toyed with Socialism are gone. Niebuhr has become a prophet of the established order of American politics in the postwar years. Nevertheless, it is a development which is consistent with his early work. Power could not be trusted unless it was set within an agreed framework of accountability. That framework needed to be open and rooted in justice and freedom. The importance of this work should not be underestimated. Politicians across the spectrum of democratic politics studied him with deep interest and sought his counsel.

Such work belonged to an age of hope about the potential for democracy and a commitment to social justice to deliver us from darkness and provide the context for individuals and communities to flourish in freedom.

The crisis of confidence in our institutions

At the end of the twentieth century there is much less certainty about these things.[4] In supposedly democratic nations many people feel alienated and distant from power. Confidence in centrally determined and universally equitable solutions is waning even in the face of democratic procedures. Government – central, local or even international – is seen as part of the problem. The optimism of the postwar years that we could build a better world in which all could exercise responsible citizenship and be treated with justice and compassion has mostly evaporated. The world has changed and we find it hard to get at the issues of community with any sense of direction.

The challenges which face us in community life today are very complex. The early part of this century was dominated by a concern about the class divisions of our society and of Western culture. The massive changes to our social and economic order brought about by industrialisation in the late eighteenth and throughout the nineteenth century shaped the experience of the first half of the twentieth century. Alongside the power vested in land and the status that went with it came the power of capital and a new class of the owners of capital. In an industrial age capital needed labour – massed labour. Capital creating new productive plant using the resource of mass labour led to the development of the industrial city and town. That led, through the process of mass industrialisation to a growth of the professional classes – the people who managed and serviced an industrial economy.

Economic and social change had created a new form of a society divided by class.

The social, political and economic distinctions between these classes lay at the centre of the political debate and struggle about the meaning of democracy. The social questions raised by a dominant industrial economy were perceived as all embracing. Class division was the challenge. In the twentieth century this was met by the extension of democratic rights to all people whatever their economic or social status. Voting was no longer restricted to property owners and to men. Full and equal rights of citizenship were given to all people. Alongside this, and as with the extension of political rights not without struggle, grew the structure of public welfare services designed to protect people from the vagaries of a market industrial economy and to remove the fears of unemployment and poverty. By that twin approach – shared citizenship and social protection – it was hoped that the divisions created by the development of industrial capitalism would be steadily overcome and the community could live in social peace.

In spite of these major and massive achievements, at the end of the twentieth century people still feel excluded from power. The persistence of poverty has been well documented in capitalist as well as Communist societies. It just does not want to go away. So the struggle to create a sense of shared obligation continues.

The issues of the division of our society between the rich and the poor have not, indeed, gone away. The evidence suggests that the gap between the richest and the poorest is larger than it has been for over a century. Our society is still divided between those who participate in its benefits and those excluded. But the analysis of this in terms of a classical understanding of class division no longer fits with the clarity that it seemed to hold in an industrialised and mass labour force society.

Society was both in Victorian times and in the earlier part of this century more complex than a straightforward class analysis suggested. But the diversity was not so obvious. The complexities and interconnecting diversities of our modern society cannot be so easily escaped. They relate to the manifest pluralism of human life today.

This has led to a look at the problems we face through much more focused questions. Diversity has particularised the work and the concern. That threatens disintegration which, in turn, undermines the possibility of an understanding and experience of place in community. But let us enter this diverse world and look at the issues with the particular focus of specific challenges. We may enter by a variety of doors.

Women and an inclusive society

Issues of gender open one such door. Poverty, for example, has a strongly feminine face. That is true across the world. Women bear the burden of poverty and the pain of the struggle to feed their households. That is as true of a village in some of the poorest parts of Africa as it is of many lone parent homes in our own society. This raises questions about whether or not we are serious about being an inclusive culture and social order.

The twentieth century has witnessed a great transition in the position of women in society. In the nineteenth century the position of women was largely defined by their place in the family. Both they and their property were viewed by the law as the property of their husband. In bourgeois society a woman found her place through marriage. The whole structure of the law surrounding marriage and domestic life undergirded the authority of men. A number of features of this culture survived deep into the twentieth century. Only in the 1980s, for example, did the taxation system stop treating married women as part of their husbands' financial order. The law has moved systematically to seeking to give women an independent and equal status in society.

It should not be assumed either that these ongoing changes will be achieved by a concept of evolutionary progress by some deterministic concept of history moving remorselessly to utopia. This is not a natural or historical progression but one that has to be continually worked at and adapted to the ever changing needs of our culture. The changes which have been made have often been won after considerable struggle – witness the campaign in the early years of the twentieth century for votes for women.

It remains a large agenda. There are matters of equal opportunity in employment and remuneration, of recognition of the needs of home life and provision for children, of the renegotiation of the way partners support and sustain one another in their several vocations. This is particularly true in matters affecting parental responsibility and how both parents are supported and enable one another in fulfilling this role. That leads on to the reshaping of attitudes and expectations, to the importance of education and to the development of social attitudes and norms of behaviour, and to language and the forms in which ideas and themes are presented. Changing actual social provision has to go hand in hand with changing attitudes in the whole of society.

These matters are complex. We do well to avoid simplistic responses. The divisions of our culture run through the community of women. The experience of poverty creates its own divisions. Contrast the struggle of lone parents, predominantly women – who feel the burden of poverty and social exclusion with the fact that the growth area in employment in recent years (and not just part-time low-paid employment but also full-time employment) has been in women's employment. The business of inclusion and exclusion cuts through the community of women in our society. These lines are fluid and open to change. The journey continues and it will have to take account of the unfinished business of the unequal experience of women in the persistence of poverty in our society.

These complexities make the task of public policy-making difficult. It is very easy for people to be confused about what is right when public policy shifts from a posture of supporting parents in the parental task to one of encouraging women to enter the labour market. These things are not mutually exclusive but the language and value framework within which they are discussed needs a lot of care.

The opportunities of a multi-cultural society

A complementary but not exactly similar story emerges when we pass through the door of issues raised by the persistence of racism in Western societies. The depth of the reality of racism becomes more obvious when we think about the difficulty we have finding a shared language for the conversation. It is difficult to talk in terms of ethnicity when many associate that language with talk about black people. Every person belongs to an ethnic group. Ethnicity is not an exclusively black experience! It is common to all people – we are brought into this world and raised in many cultural settings and with different and complementary histories. So immediately we hit the problem of language in our culture and how it may serve the purposes of inclusion and the protection and nurture of the equal dignity and place of every person and every community. We have not even got a way of speaking about one another which affirms and upholds the integrity of all.

Political correctness may be attacked in the popular mind but the journey of finding a way of speaking which a diverse community is able to own and which is seen to be affirmative of every person's integrity is not easy. In matters which touch the heart of our being language has to be owned. We must be in charge of how we are addressed. Even our language is having to adjust to the changing needs of communication in the modern world. It is particularly difficult when people find sweeping generalities in language offensive. If we are not to move into a babel world of many different languages which those outside do not and cannot understand we have got to go on working together at how we may speak of and to one another. The doing of this task has to be inclusive.

The complexity of racism can be seen in the particular. In Surrey there are two communities which manifestly evidence the multi-cultural and multi-ethnic character of our society. There is a lively Islamic community living predominantly in Woking whose roots are in the Indian sub-continent. People are frequently surprised to hear that it is in Surrey – in Woking – that the oldest mosque in Britain is to be found. Muslim people have offered their worship to God here for over one hundred years in this town. The other centres of multi-ethnicity in Surrey are our prisons. There are four prisons in the county.

The paradoxical nature of these two contexts brings many of the questions to the surface. The cross-cultural and multi-faith issues raised by the community of our Muslim brothers and sisters give us a way into the challenges of a pluralistic society. The experience of black people in relation to the law gives another about discrimination and exclusion.

The community of the mosque is a strong local community made up predominantly, but not exclusively, of families who came to the United Kingdom from Pakistan. The bonds of faith are reinforced by the bonds of family and community culture. The mosque and its people are part of contemporary Britain. As with every community different sorts of relationship are struck up with other communities. There are tentative but not unfriendly links with the churches. There are shared concerns and experience of local services. Education and nurture are high priorities for Muslim families which they share with many others. Members of this community make a contribution to the economic health of their local community. People come to depend on the services offered.

Misunderstanding and occasional unreconstructed racist action remind all of the importance of building community and that the task is still being negotiated. The mosque has been attacked and its members feel the stereotyping of Islam in our culture. Yet friendship and good trusted lines of communication enable a now well-established community to contribute to the welfare of all. The attitudes and understanding of all have to change if we are to contribute to their well-being. A culture of mutuality is gradually rooted in the heart of the whole community. Again, these changes do not happen naturally. They have to be chosen and worked upon in the face of a reluctance to accept the changes needed for an open and inclusive future. We have to construct a different way of seeing the oneness of our community. That must embrace its diversity.

On the front line of the second context are the police and the structures of law enforcement in Britain today. The presence of large numbers of black people in our prisons is evidence of a persistent difficulty. The police, the legal profession, the courts and behind them the dominant culture of social expectation and attitudes towards crime in our society are the field on which the unresolved issues of racism are fought. The presence of so many black people in prison threatens a racist divide. We run the risk of the criminalisation of a community. The presence of so many black young men in prison and the absence of black people from the various law enforcement agencies make for a dangerously unresolved matter.

Moreover this represents a construct of our world which may have little relation to the needs and desires of people for a peaceful and open society. Community can only be built on the presumption that people do want to live at peace with their neighbours. That requires confidence-building measures between the different faces of our community today and the institutions whose task it is to help us live at peace with each other. How do we deconstruct a world which threatens to criminalise some and scapegoat minority communities for the ills of the whole of society? This is the task we have found so difficult to face, let alone tackle.

Again, the issues are multi-faceted. Different communities have different histories, sometimes different religious and social norms, and this creates misunderstanding and tension which is exacerbated by racism.

Family life today

Contemporary household life offers another door into the diversity of community life today. We will deal with the detail of this in a later chapter. The widespread commitment to the importance of family is expressed in a colourful variety of domestic order from the traditional nuclear household, through to same-sex households. People live together in permanent or semi-permanent relationships inside and outside of marriage and in heterosexual or same-sex relationships. They may or may not have the responsibility of the care of children or of elderly relatives and close friends.

The needs are as varied as the forms of domestic life today. The task of ensuring fairness, of protecting the vulnerable and enabling people to fulfil the responsibilities of the relationships they have taken on belie simple legal or social solutions. This diversity has encouraged a targeting of social provision. The needs of children, for example, are specifically provided for in the historic and important Children Act. The responsibilities of parents in providing for their children is tackled separately in the provision of the controversial Child Support Agency. It is all very specific. There is much to be said for it. The problem lies in consistency. Are there common and unifying values which inform the specific character of the provision?

A child is abused by his or her father. The man is then prosecuted and given a custodial sentence. All very laudable since children have a particular right to be safe in their families. The consequences are far-reaching. The marriage breaks down. The family is broken up. The family home is sold. The child who is the victim suffers further and profound losses. A parent is lost, a home is lost, a family is broken. The act of abuse leads not just to the awfulness of the violation of the child but to the collapse of many worlds which the child may depend on for security and confidence. Yet the law is supposed to work for the interests of the child.

A marriage breaks down and father abandons home for

another partner leaving a mother to bring up two small children. The father fails to make adequate financial provision for his children. He is chased by the Child Support Agency for substantial sums for their support. That support is set against the benefit being paid to the mother – now a lone parent without employment. The mother is no better off and is made dependent on the father producing his share. The family is no better off and bitterness has been added to bitterness. A commitment to support family responsibility ends up in greater stress.

The laudable endeavour at holding on to human values and emphasising the responsibilities of parenting children in the midst of the plurality of people's lifestyles is not easy. We still have a lot of work to do to put the pieces together in ways which protect individuals, underline mutual responsibility and build rather than destroy the communities of life on which we all depend for our security.

So we have to go on putting the diverse pieces together through a coherent set of social values which protects each part from the disorder threatened by a lack of integrated social thought.

Dangers in single issue politics

This kaleidoscopic experience has encouraged a single issue approach to the community task. Modern political life is like an orchestra tuning up – a cacophany of sound waiting to find some semblance of order and structure. Groups of citizens are consumed with the task of stopping the building of this or that road, winning equality of opportunity and rights, banning guns or protecting the country way of life. Many instruments begin to tune up. In the background are a variety of concepts of freedom and the rights and responsibilities of individuals and local communities. Noises are heard from the deep notes of the brass section giving hope of some musical coherence. But the music scripts are not related to each other and each part of the orchestra threatens to play to the beat it finds

121

most congenial. Then just as the conductor seeks to bring order the NIMBY syndrome hits the drums. We are not playing if the trumpets are allowed to stay in the orchestra. Not In My Back Yard. That is the difficulty of a postmodern culture which pays no heed to the essential structures of our shared life which make it possible for all to play. Community never gets going as the different parts fail to see the importance of making the music work in harmony for all.

It makes the community building task very hard and the political vocation very frustrating. The whole thing sometimes seems to stand on the brink of breaking down.

The impact of contemporary communications

The revolution in communications has made the world smaller. Not only is the local community made up of people of many cultures and lifestyles it is also much more likely to be in touch with other parts of the world. In business it is possible to create a new design in Britain, transfer it by modern technology to a country like India where production can begin. All will be financed from an international money market. At one and the same time the world has been drawn into ever closer relationship and made much more aware of its great variety and flexibility. No local or national community can live to itself. The attempt leads to death. Every attempt at bucking the system, however well intentioned, is doomed. Julius Nyerere's principled endeavour at creating a rural socialist economy in the newly independent Tanzania fell apart because it could not escape the power of the economic forces at work in an international economy. These developments are leading to the creation of political structures which keep pace with the changing realities of the international economy. Federalism between nation states is growing as a way of enabling international co-operation and creating powerful political agencies capable of responding to the forces at work in the economy.

Federal forces bring local forces to life. If power has run

outwards to the international field it has also run inwardly towards more localised politics. How else can we cope with the diverse needs of a plural world? Subsidiarity has become an important principle of modern politics – decisions must be taken by the people as close to the issue as is reasonably possible and practicable. That is aimed at the diverse needs of people by ensuring that they have immediate control over the immediate matters of their own corporate life. This requires a new sense of co-operation between different levels of power. No one body can carry the power for all. Power has to be diffused across society if meaningful and acceptable decisions are to be made for our common life.

Even at the local level that process of diversity and attending to the needs of local groups and networks of associations is gathering pace. Services are devolved out of town halls into neighbourhoods. New skills are having to be learnt about consultation and interpretation of local need to enable judgements to be made which will lead to different outcomes in different settings. The exact nature of the education offered in one school may not be the same as what is considered to be appropriate in the neighbouring areas. The character of health provision will be shaped to the more exact sense of need as determined by the local users. It is a difficult world and one which is going to require new political skills. Values of trust, of an acceptance of agreed standards of conduct and process for all, social auditing and accountability will be the watchwords of democracy in this more diverse and pluralistic framework of people's lives.

The values emerge from the experience of making sense of our diversity. Commonality is not arrived at by centrally imposed norms but by the persistent reflection on the way we are all performing our civic duty. This bottom up approach requires a deeper sense of civic responsibility across the whole community. Politics has become too serious an issue to leave to the politicians. It has to be a shared task requiring a more direct involvement of the people in their several communities. Those to whom we entrust political authority have to learn ways of exercising it which are open to public participation and are flexible in the face of real public accountability. This is the challenge of the new politics in democratic societies. It is this sort of a process which will enable a diverse community to grow together rather than fracture into separated pieces.

Since there are many places in our world which seem to be able to manage diversity only by division, it is vital that those who have the opportunity of working on alternative and more inclusive models should have the courage to make the journey. In places like South Africa all the help and support of others is needed to cement the foundations of a new and inclusive order which flourishes on the diversity of its cultural history. The same sort of issues are nearer to us in the search for resolution in Ireland – which we explore elsewhere.

These major constitutional issues in which people are trying to make human sense of a divided and conflictual history illustrate the fundamental importance of the political and constitutional task in the contemporary world. How we construct and sustain civic life for the benefit of the people leads us into far-reaching questions about the significance of our humanity. The challenge is spiritual and political – about the meaning of human life in community and about the form given to that in the modern world.

Too much of our recent history has been dominated by economics. That is not the fault of those who engage in such activity. It is what happens when there is a vacuum in the realm of political thought. Politics requires us to put some shape on the meaning of our humanity in community. It requires us to make visible what we believe. Its practical solutions arise out of vision. It is not just a forum for the struggle of power but a medium by which we decide how we intend to live as neighbours. That is critical when neighbours live such different and divergent sorts of lives.

If power is constructed – as the postmodernist might suggest – then the door is open for us to consider from what perspective we want to construct the operation of political power for the future. If things are neither the result of the fates nor the inevitable outworking of the forces of progress in history, they are open to the choices we make. Pluralism and diversity do not inevitably mean a bare struggle for power between sectional and partisan interests. It does not have to end up either in chaos and darkness as each retreats into their own private world or in the triumph of the powerful over the rest. We can covenant to live in peace on the basis of respect for each other's journey of faith and humanity allowing the future to emerge out of the enjoyment of the present.

None would suggest that that is easy or that it does not require acts of political courage and even of sacrifice. The constructs which arise out of such visions and humanity not only offer hope to all people but their roots go deep because they reflect the eternal realities which sustain us all.

Life in the Home

Jane Austen with a gentle but incisive caricature sent up the middle-class family culture of her time. Mrs Bennett, that neurotic but persistent seeker for husbands for her congregation of daughters, brings a smile to our twentieth-century faces. A woman needed to be well-married to find her proper place in society. In Victorian Britain the dominance of a particular culture of marriage and family reached its height. In law women had little or no status outside of marriage and little right of their own within it. They and their property were firmly in the hands of their husbands. The twentieth century has, progressively, seen the tide run out on this culture of domestic life. Old bourgeois values and institutions have been first questioned, then challenged and finally replaced.

The family and marriage after two world wars

The Beveridge Report,[1] which provided the framework for the post 1945 Welfare State, had an inbuilt weakness. It had an outdated view of the shape and meaning of the family in postwar Britain. In his famous Report the idea of services from the cradle to the grave revolved around the traditional view of the family: two parents living in a permanent married state bringing up their own natural children. Father would be the breadwinner, mother the housewife and child rearer. Housing policy, benefits policy, pensions policy, taxation policy were all geared to the model. Whilst on the surface it seemed to be a reasonable model to work with – after all most people lived in such homes – underneath the changes were already beginning to gather momentum. Looking from

1945 forward it was possible to understand that the future was going to be different. That future would not involve the abolition of the natural family. It would, however, lead to the growth of other and complementary forms of domestic relationship alongside the traditional shape of family order. Household and family life would remain strong but different.

A number of things had already happened in British society which pointed to this more diverse future. The terrible carnage of the First World War had robbed the nation of a large part of a generation of young men and so left a society lacking in balance between the sexes. A generation of single women had to provide for themselves. As Pat Barker has brought to the surface in her poignant and powerful trilogy on the First World War[2] it had a profound effect on the way people understood themselves and their culture. The meaning of gender and sexuality and their relationship to class was irreversibly changed for the millions caught up in this terrible war. These shifts of understanding added fuel to the struggle of women in the twentieth century for equal rights and for their humanity not to be defined by their marital status. The demographic realities of Britain after 1918 went hand in hand with the other forces at work demanding change for women.

The Second World War shifted experience in the economic order. Women took on roles in the productive life of the nation which had previously been closed to them. The necessity of war demanded real change. After the war ended men returned to their former roles in a programme which returned people to the work they had before they had been enlisted in the forces. That went hand in hand with a drive to recreate traditional family life. However, the experience could not be taken away. As prosperity increased in the 1950s and 60s growing numbers of women, both married and single, who had made considerable progress in achieving equality of opportunity in education, sought a stake of their own in the modern economy. That momentum continues. In our own time the real growth in full-time employment has been in the sphere of women's employment. That means many households have come to be double income households in which roles need to be shared by both men and women if the home and family are to work.

Sadly, these changes have gone alongside the collapse of full employment. As some homes and families have succeeded in making it into the modern economy so a considerable minority have been shut out. Some households have no members in income earning work. Real divisions have opened up between those with good income and those living in poverty. The feminine face of poverty is particularly acute in the homes where there is no paid work. This is especially so in households where the woman is the lone parent trying to both fulfil the role of parent and to ensure that the home has enough income to meet its needs.

So in many respects the Beveridge model of household life is no longer pertinent. Economic trends have had a profound impact on the way families order their lives. That has required considerable adjustment in the way help is brought by the public purse to individuals and families at time of need. We still struggle to find an efficient, humane, flexible and people orientated benefits system.

The erosion of marriage

The changes, however, have gone much further and were accelerated by the nation's experience of a second war. War is deeply disruptive of family life. It was Karl Barth who said that war encourages people to break all God's commandments.[3] Men went off to the fight leaving behind them women and children. Many did not come back. Others returned so changed by the experience that neither they nor their spouses could make their relationship work again. It was not surprising, therefore, that after 1945 the divorce rate rose. Marriages were failing and the parties wanted to be out of it. Pressure grew for the establishment of a more humane and dignified law of divorce. In 1966 the Church of England produced a report *Putting Asunder*[4] which suggested a new basis

128

for the law of divorce in our society. The sole ground for divorce should be 'the irretrievable breakdown of the marriage'. It further suggested that we should move away from a fault-based approach to divorce proceedings. The principle of the irretrievable breakdown of the marriage as the sole ground for divorce was accepted in the 1969 Act. All subsequent history of the law of divorce from then until now has been one of making sense of that principle. However, the law did not remove fault from the process until the 1996 Act.

It is clear that the law was responding to deeper social and cultural pressures. The growth of divorce, as a way of resolving serious marital difficulty, has been a marked feature of the postwar world in Britain. Today approximately 40 per cent of marriages in Britain end in divorce and that represents one of the highest rates across Europe. Whatever judgement we make of this it has clearly changed the way people approach and understand marriage. It has also had a profound impact on household living.

The outcomes, as we have experienced them, include a growth in lone parent households. Many women, in particular, having gone through divorce are left to bring up their children alone and are cautious about seeking another marriage. Twenty-two per cent of families in our society are headed by lone parents. This is three times the proportion of 1971. Some do enter into reasonably permanent new relationships – inside or outside of marriage – and form new households. Significant numbers of children in these second or reconstituted families continue to relate to their natural parents (50 per cent of fathers living apart from their children see them at least once a week) as well as to the present partner of the parent with whom they are living. Family relationships have become more complex and diverse.[5]

The sexual revolution

Into this cauldron of change we must add the sexual revolution of the twentieth century. The development and widespread use of artificial means of contraception has had a profound effect upon people's attitude to sexual relationships. The consequent changes in both married and family experience are considerable. The sexual act is no longer so closely tied, in people's minds and experience, to procreation. Having children is much more a choice people make and can control. Child-bearing can be planned.

Sex is much safer than it used to be. There is less practical reason for tying sex to marriage provided couples take the necessary precautions. The majority of couples who get married have lived together before marriage (68 per cent). Many choose not to enter marriage at all. For some cohabitation has become a reasonably permanent way of life. Thirty-four per cent of children are born outside of marriage and 80 per cent of these births are registered by both parents. One of the results of this is that the numbers of people getting married have fallen dramatically – 50 per cent of the level of a generation ago.[6]

So many households will be made up of people not married or who have been married and are now no longer so. Marriage, traditionally understood, is not the dominant institution it was fifty years ago. Contraception has loosened the bond between sexual union, child-bearing and marriage. Marriage is still a pivotal and defining institution for home life but it is by no means the exclusive pattern of the way people form strong and mutually supportive relationships.

In looking at the challenges to the traditional understanding of marriage and family life we also have to recognise the growth of alternative lifestyles such as those of the gay and lesbian communities. 'Safe sex' makes it possible for people to choose different lifestyles. All these matters raise contemporary and perplexing issues of principle – what is 'good', and 'right'. Complementary questions concerning the meaning of justice and stability in domestic life – how we can treat people with equity and equal dignity – are similarly raised to the surface by these shifts in our culture and practice.

So Beveridge's Dad at work, Mum at home, two to three

children resulting from their union, supported by a strong system of public welfare and so living in security, is a world little known to increasing numbers of people today.

The family remains strong

So household life has changed – and radically. That, however, does not mean to say that the experience of family is in crisis. There is plenty of evidence to show that people look to their homes for a wide range of support and as places where they can find security and love. Married, divorced or cohabiting parents are committed to their children. Young people are living at home longer than in the past. People profess to stronger ties with their families than with their friends. Although mobility has spread the family more widely across the world it seems that adult children exercise considerable responsibility towards their aging parents and relatives. It is the shape and form of household living which has shifted not the sense of commitment to its importance.

These changes do present real challenges both to the Church and to the whole community. There are very real difficulties in maintaining sufficient clarity and stability around the structure of our domestic living. These do threaten the widespread desire for the home to be an effective guardian of loving security for both adults and children. A lack of confidence in marriage and a lack of clarity about parental relationships and obligations undermine family life. The other side of every person knowing their place – who is living with whom and who is responsible for whom – is that each person knows where they belong. Family life is rooted in confidence in belonging. People turn almost instinctively to their homes for support and protection in time of stress and uncertainty. This is where each person belongs and the moment of crisis reveals it. It is a very serious lack when individuals are not clear where they belong. This is one of the reasons why homelessness and refugee experience is so debilitating and degrading. It attacks an essential need for belonging.

The changes in our household life in the last decades have put strains on the inherited structure and understanding of marriage and of some aspects of family life. They have not, however, undermined our human capacity to make our homes places of love and security for the vast majority of their members. The crisis relates to the construct we place upon family life not on family life itself. That is why so many people do not understand Christians when they try and justify the inherited structure for marriage as the only one which delivers strong home life. The strength and quality of people's relationships seem to matter a great deal more in the day-to-day business of home life. It is certainty about one's place in the home which is crucial for the stability of adults and children forming a modern family.

Returning to first principles

Rethinking the place and form of marriage in contemporary family life requires us to return to some basic principles so that we can construct a more helpful way of understanding this critical institution and make appropriate provision for it both in society and in people's expectations of it. Although a great deal of the Churches' work on marriage has been done in relation to the vexed issues of divorce and subsequent second or further marriages, we would do well to consider marriage for its own sake and then look at what this might mean today.

Three theological and pastoral principles might help us begin.

First, Christians have always taught that marriage is a gift from God in creation and is, therefore, a blessing on human life. Seeing marriage as rooted in God's goodness in creation – part of the confidence we can have in the universe – means that it is closely allied to our human need. We can experience it as a good thing. Something has gone wrong if a culture sees marriage as a burden and a bad thing in experience. Because it is a gift of God and good and something which relates well to what we as created beings need for a life of growth and freedom, it is not something to be seen and presented as an imposition which we have to knuckle under and endure. Marriage which has to be endured is not the gift which is given by God. When things go wrong all the blame should not necessarily fall on the parties. There might be important lessons for the construct we have in our minds of marriage and family.

Second, marriage is a means of grace. As a gift of God it is a vehicle by which God brings goodness and mercy to bear on our human life. Traditionally we have thought of this as affecting two people who are married to each other. But that is not the limit of marriage as a means of grace. Through the experience of a good marriage blessing and goodness are brought to the whole community. So the institution of marriage in society and our experience of it are meant to be good for all people. Again, if the experience of marriage in our social and cultural order is not one of something good then the culture is falling short of the gift and goodness of God.

Third, marriage is a vocation. The sense of being called to it affirms the critical need for consent by both parties to the contract. Marriage is not to be imposed but received freely and thankfully by the parties as a good gift.

Marriage as vocation reminds us that not all people are called to enter the married state. Its blessings and its goodness are open to all people and should be felt by the whole community. There is no suggestion, however, that it is appropriate for all people to enter marriage. So whatever the social context within which we shape our domestic life it is always going to have to take account of the needs of those not married. The twentieth century has moved progressively away from a culture of expectation that everyone should get married. That has made us consider the needs of those who are not called to be married. Clearly that includes those who have been bereaved or abandoned. It also includes those who never come to marriage and who see not being married as a vocation. Included among these people are many for whom marriage would be wholly inappropriate. The tragedy for some gay people is that, for the sake of finding a place in the social order, they have sought marriage. It is usually disastrous. Marriage has to be a vocation not a social demand.

It is worth our noting that in different generations and different social settings people have sought to find their place in the community as people who are not married. That may be a temporary or a more permanent state. Some become part of large extended families and households. Others enter different forms of ordered community – including religious community. Occasionally people accept a vocation to the solitary life as hermits. For the sake of friendship and community people share homes and support one another by such means. Other vocations can sometimes provide a sense of location for people who are not married, for example residential institutions such as schools, the armed forces, caring agencies. For periods of people's lives some sense of belonging and mutual care is enabled by such means.

A society which values the institution of marriage as pivotal for its health will find plenty of space for enabling all people to form appropriate community life under its broad umbrella. There is no blueprint for this, just a recognition that the changing circumstances of our culture will always have such a need. We must not see the fact that significant numbers of people choose, at least for periods of their life, not to be married as a threat to God's gift. God's gift was never meant to be a universal imposition.

What is good about marriage?

There are three broad goods to marriage.

The first is about union and communion. This is a gift of God to provide for intimate communion between the two sexes. Men and women are made for each other and are

134

drawn to share their lives together. That is focused on the relationship of one man and one woman together who are joined to form what Christians have described as 'one flesh'. In this relationship people discover something of the meaning of true love. That love unites them in ever deepening ways. The spiritual secret which unlocks the meaning of such love is the love which constantly gives itself away to others. So the bond of marriage is one of mutual giving and receiving. Each holds something of the secret of the life of the other. Built within its heart is the conviction that marriage is exclusive and monogamous, and is a covenant and bond for life. This is the quality of the relationship. Two people in a bond of love and mutuality grow together. In growing together they also grow as individuals. Their life together becomes a context for personal growth and for growing freedom and maturity.

Any structure of marriage which undermines that basic aspect of our humanity corrupts it. It is always open to corruption. Understandings of marriage which spin round the power of men are corrupt and undermine the credibility of the institution. Historically wives have been viewed as their husbands' property and only having rights by derivation of their status as wives. A hierarchical view of authority has threatened to reduce marriage to a battleground between the sexes. If women and men are to feel confident in this relationship it will need to be constructed as a partnership and contract between two people of equal right and dignity. It will have to be ordered to meet the diverse needs of its parties in the contemporary world. Imposed and out of date cultures are doomed to disaster and will only further reduce the significance of marriage in our time. If marriage is to succeed women will need to feel secure within it and men will need to accept the disciplines of a shared enterprise. Marriage is essentially a union of two people within a communion of shared life and love.

The second good of marriage is that it is a creative relationship. That is focused on the gift of children. The lack of children, however, in no way invalidates a marriage. The creative consequences of marriage are for the parties and for their families and communities. The creative energy in people's lives takes on a special meaning in the creation of new life and its nurture and growth. This is fundamental to being part of a living world and it is an expression of the meaning of love for persons made in the image of the divine creator. Just as at a personal level marriage tells the community what sort of a relationship two people are in and consequently what our obligations are to them, so it provides a secure and understood context for the nurture of children. That task is not exclusive – it will always be shared with others – but it is pivotal.

And it is a shared enterprise. The growing awareness in our own society that both parents have obligations to children they produce or take into their care is a point of good growth. Each parent will contribute different things to the way their children grow. We must be careful not to stereotype fathering or mothering. It is a complementary responsibility which, in the mystery of the uniqueness of each person, will subtly vary from person to person, marriage to marriage, child to child and community to community. The interplay of social and economic necessity, personality and family experience is a mix capable of producing a kaleidoscope of ways in which families organise themselves around the parental task.

The growing sense of the importance of family life for the health of our society means that it has to be taken into account in the constructing of the wider social realities. The idea, for example, that employers have a right to drain every last drop of human energy out of their employees and return them to their homes incapable of offering anything creative to the task of home building is socially destructive. The modern world needs balance between the different settings of human vocation. One of the things the growth of employment amongst married women might achieve is a rising concern to balance patterns of economic and working life with the needs of home life. Where there are unresolved conflicts of interest we have to learn to strike the sort of compromises which keep vocation alive across the full range of our humanity.

Oppressive societies make little provision for these things. Apartheid took men away from their local communities to meet the economic demands of the powerful interests in South Africa. The desperate experience of hostel life in the townships included the degrading of the vocation of these people as fathers and husbands and members of families and local communities. The way economic life destroys family life is often a sign of an oppressive as opposed to a liberated society. All societies live somewhere on the spectrum between these extremes. The test of their vibrancy is their capacity to face up to and work on the potential points of oppression. Enabling both men and women to engage in creative and income-earning work in society and fulfil their parental and family responsibilities is one such point of test in our society.

The third good of marriage is its capacity to provide a focus for community life. Homes and families are community-building institutions. In the immediate they provide support for the extended family. They are the front line of care for members of the family. People go to their family when they are in need or distress or facing uncertainty. Again, this is not exclusive to marriages. These goods are experienced in a variety of ways in our world. Yet it is clear that marriage remains and is likely to remain critical to this experience.

In the encouraging of a sense of openness about the home for their children and their children's friends, in the hospitality and care offered to the wider family and in the home becoming a place for neighbours to meet and find hospitality and support, a married couple make their home a community-building place. That blessing runs off into all forms of community life and household living.

Marriage becomes, thereby, a public institution and not just a private arrangement between the parties. One of the problems we have faced in our own culture has been the privatising of marriage. It is presented as an exclusive and private contract between the two parties with little or no sense of the public nature of the event and of the arrangement. The home that is created for the couple is seen as a sort of small castle – a place of refuge from the modern world. The security of the home becomes a driving concern. How to keep people out rather than how people are able to come in. Of course it requires a sense of balance. No home can be so taken over by even the children let alone the community that the couple lose control of it. It is their home. As their home it is an opportunity for them to contribute to the wider well-being of the community. We have a lot to learn about the importance of hospitality, the symbolic power of the meal table as a place where we learn and grow through the mutual exchange of our lives.

For Christians that open and engaging understanding of marriage and family life – as a sign which works itself into all forms of household community – is also a place of spiritual nurture. A house is a church. Those responsible for it are ministers of the good things God gives to all in Christ. Again, this is not exclusive. There are some who make the serious mistake of thinking that the parents alone are responsible for all their children's education and spiritual nurture. The whole church and the wider community have equally vital contributions to make so that each person grows to be the unique person God seeks and not just a clone of their parents! Nevertheless, the home is a place of spiritual nurture. Here people learn to pray, to give thanks, to offer their loves and griefs to God and to break bread together within the love of God for all. Here people learn the shape of the faith and the hard graft of making it work in their lives. The home is one of the places where the Church needs to encourage the practice of the faith outside the four walls of the Sunday life of the worshipping community. We need help in enabling this to happen.

A blessing for all?

Marriage becomes a sign and symbol of what is for all. This is where we need to work on what this might mean for the diversity of household life as we have it today. It is not good for anyone to live alone. Whatever vocations people discover we need each other. However we structure our lives we need the community of others and we need close community with others. If marriage is the witness to that in the world it need not be seen as the exclusive deliverer of it.

People form close community in many ways and these are important. For example, people need the friendship and communion of their own sex. Marriage alters the character of such relationships but does not destroy the need. We find critical and important support systems within the communities of our own sex. It is possible that the shift away from the dominant position held by marriage in the century from the mid-nineteenth century to the postwar period is a necessary righting of a balance we had lost. Friendship, comradeship, sisterhood are not to be seen as negative comments on the adequacy of marriage but a part of what it means to be human.

We begin to stray into more controversial country when we start to explore the meaning of our sexuality in these contexts. Whatever the unresolved issues we might at least acknowledge some important common ground. By relating all domestic community to what marriage is about in the divine gift we are setting ourselves real and humanly defined boundaries. These boundaries make sense of the story of Divine Revelation. So we can resist that sort of loose libertarianism which suggests that anything goes. Clearly, what must be encouraged is what builds community, gives people security and enables each person to find a wholesome and sustaining place in society. All of us could work on what that means for different people.

Furthermore we would do well to recognise that sexuality is not just a part of being human. It is an essential dimension of all humanity. Sex is a window into understanding who we are. Not the only window but one of the ones which is part of the essential nature of our being human persons. To suggest, therefore, that there is a sexual dimension to all our relationships and that it is good to give thought to what this means is not to support anything corrupt or ungodly. Those who have chosen the way of chastity as their vocation do so not as a denial of their sexuality but as an affirmation of what it means for them. Those who choose paths of life as a way of escape from aspects of the human run risks that what they suppress will emerge in destructive ways when they are ill prepared to deal with them.

So we have to be positive. Denial will not do. The Christian understanding of who we are as persons made in the image of God requires us to make positive provision for living out our faith in all sides of our humanity. People who, for example, find that their sexual orientation is gay or lesbian and who are Christian cannot simply be told to suppress their humanity and deny it. All of us have to be positive about our sexuality and the decisions each person makes about how to express that have to affirm the God-given nature of our essential humanity.

It is at this point that the pastoral task of the Church and the maintaining of a creative and inclusive social order interact. The Church has rather a better record of achievement in this area than sometimes is allowed. The work done, for example, in Anglicanism on the moral issues raised by family planning is an example of the way the pastoral needs of the people – including church people – provided a driving force for some fresh thinking. The eventual acceptance of the use of artificial means of contraception as a positive good for married couples represented a vital development in moral theology keeping theology and pastoral practice in close relation to each other.[7] The other good example is one already referred to, namely the work done by Bishop Mortimer's group in the report, *Putting Asunder*.[8] Here pastoral practice and social provision were interactive. A major statement of the theology of marriage in the public forum and in the context of the pastoral issues of the mid-twentieth century has created a foundation for all subsequent ecclesiastical and social thought within the Anglican tradition.

These two examples encourage us in continuing to work in this interactive manner in facing the moral and personal challenges of a world in which marriage is pivotal but not exclusive to people's family and home life. If we do so we will have to work progressively seeking to respond to the pastoral challenges of people's needs for stable and creative domestic living today and bringing their experience into the heart of the theological task. The challenges are hard because they involve making sense of sexually active relationships outside of marriage – both cohabiting couples and gay and lesbian people in sexually active partnerships. Similar sorts of discussion and work are going on in other cultures still struggling with making pastoral sense of the life of people living in polygamous relationships. As with them so with us we are talking about the personal and spiritual growth of members of the Christian Church. The Christian gospel has taken root in many different communities and has certainly taken root across the diversity of our own postmodern sort of culture.

How are we going to tackle the task? Not by rushing to the difficulties and battling it out in the hope that one point of view or another might win. If we think of our household and family life as pictured by a house, we should resist the temptation of rushing in through the door and up to the bedroom. Finding a way of constructing our life today which is consonant with our Christian inheritance and makes sense to people of faith trying to bring some order and meaning to their lives requires a more holistic and measured approach. We need to consider the house as a whole. How well designed is it – what adjustments might be made in the basic design which might fit it for the needs of today and the future? Just the sort of discussion about marriage in a pluralistic society we have been starting here. Then we can progress inside the house and see how the shape of household life being considered meets the diverse but fundamental needs of people for security, community, personal growth, spiritual development, service to the wider networks of family and neighbourhood, hospitality and nurture of the needy. Then we might gently and carefully consider how such people show their love to one another as whole human beings.

By such means we make the journey forward and recognise the essential truth of Christian life that we all have to change and that the journey is not yet complete. What comes out of this wrestling with principle and practice in the future will both have a consonance with the past and be something new as well. By such means the story goes on and the Good News remains good in a changing culture.

For our own immediate culture the unresolved questions in this area of our life cause us the most difficulty in responding to the diversity of our time. These matters are alive within the community of faith as people with very different stories to tell seek to learn the meaning of the vision of God for the choices they are required to make in the construct of their lives. Love working for freedom unites without being repressive. It calls for all to be open both in the shaping of a good community and in the receiving of what others bring to the task. The process of moral and social construction is, therefore, critical to the discernment of truth.

What we do know is that truth will appeal to all who in faith and good conscience are pursuing the vision of love moving towards freedom.

Art and the Meaning of Prophecy in the Twentieth Century

'Who has been telling the truth?' A critical question for discerning the prophetic word. This is a very difficult question for the Church. To come to terms with the possibility that the truth has been told by others can be very threatening. Yet, it is at the heart of the twentieth century. If truth is the crucial question for the arts, as it ought to be for the Church, then the interconnections between them should be of special interest. It will require special courage and imagination for these two worlds to speak once again to each other. How does art connect with matters of the Spirit?

The world of theology has been lost to ordinary people. It has developed a language and mode of expression which has cacooned it and detached it from the life of the people. Yet, theology is an endeavour people make, using the weakness of human language and thought, to express what they experience and understand of God. The experience of God is extensive – well beyond the borders of the Church, let alone the faculties of theology. Good theology makes it possible for all who search for God to articulate their vision and experience. Because the limitations of the task are to do with the limitations of language rather than any sense of restriction on the realities of which language tries to speak, the words used are always paradoxical, symbolic and inviting those who listen to inhabit new horizons.

Theology is never complete. It is continually aware of the desperate risk of the task – the risk of destroying the sense of mystery essential to its being. Risk is something all people know in the business of negotiating human life – from the risks of relationship to the risk of exploring the meaning of existence. We humans live with an open and unpredictable future before us.

In this, the theologian and the artist move in similar worlds. Symbolism, paradox and the subtle invitation to the inward journey of understanding are the signposts on the way of artistic creativity. The task is never complete and runs the risk of appalling idolatry – the deceit of thinking the truth is contained in what has been created. Corrupt art – art which shores up the abuses of the present – is always idolatrous.

Like art, theology is a science. It requires attention to detail and the lifelong development of precise skills. The development of these is not to create an elite but to enable artist or theologian to speak with as much clarity as is possible. Thus our imagination and inner life may be stimulated and fed and opened to things beyond the immediate. That is the way of freedom. Art, like theology, can be a liberator of human life.

So the two interconnect. Theology is a discipline of the Church. Its subject matter, however, is not primarily Church but God, humanity, world – expressed as being, truth, love, nature. Specifically Christian theology speaks of these things in response to what we have seen and experienced in Jesus Christ. In this person and this story people discover the heart of all being and the love which works for freedom.

Theology and the arts can express themselves in many ways. Three specifically theological words might embrace them both and help us find the rich food the interplay of these two worlds might produce.

Prophecy

Risk-taking theology and art are potentially prophetic. They become a challenge to the corruptions and abuse, the half-truths and injustices of our humanity. Bonhoeffer, theologian and pastor, and Shostakovich, humanist and musician, with extraordinary courage used their skill to confront the terror of the Nazi and Stalinist states. Sometimes the person who speaks directly about God offers the insight which unveils the full truth. Sometimes the artist is the lonely prophet despised by the establishment but vindicated by history.

Priestly symbolism

Priests are supposed to make connections for others. Theology and art can bring separated worlds together. That can also be liberating in the face of oppression – the oppression of the spirit or the oppression of the community. The story is sometimes told of the way the first Russian Christians toured the then Christian world to discover how to shape the life and worship of the Church. They found their answer in the great Cathedral of St Sophia in Constantinople where the liturgy transported them between earth and heaven. They did not know, so it is reported, whether they were in heaven or on earth. Art can similarly move us from one world to another. Seeing a Picasso or Rembrandt, listening to Bach or Britten can open the inner eye and help us make vital connections. That is the point where both theology and art connect with worship.

Story-telling

Theology tells a story – the good story of the unfolding of the mystery of God in the heart of our humanity. In the story those who hear are drawn into the drama, the scene, the company of the characters. That is what the gospel story told in liturgy and in the Word does in the Church. Art, which is rooted in the deep things of our being, tells us a story and draws us into its heart. Standing in front of the amazing black Madonna in St George's Cathedral, Capetown, the individual is drawn into the heart and life of black women who endured the long years of the struggle with so much pain and loss and yet dignity. Sitting in Sheffield Cathedral but weeks before the outbreak of the Gulf War in 1991 listening to Vaughan

Williams' music the silence was alive. It told a story which made us confront a story which seemed to threaten us all.

Because theology is about God and humanity and only consequentially about the Church we should not allow the mystery of the faith of some and the unbelief of others to prevent us hearing what all might have to say. The question in front of serious life-transforming theology and art is the question of truth. On that journey we might yet support one another at a moment of profound need in our history.

The prophetic tradition

If we return to examine the biblical tradition of prophetic life there are a number of aspects which might illuminate our task. Prophets were often perceived as coming from outside. Indeed, it was probably essential that they did because their words of divine judgement were directed towards those on the inside! Not only were they perceived as outsiders their words were seen as a threat to tradition and to the authority of the formal leaders of the people both in politics and religion. There was no comfort for the establishment in their life and words.

The tension of their role was made the sharper by their own sense of being one with the people. Inside their heart was an indestructible bond of love and humanity which held them to the people. Rejected they might be, but they knew themselves to belong with the people and so the hardness of the word and the hurt of rejection went deep. It was out of that intense experience, however, that the truth was more fully revealed. So their own personal experience became part of the story. Politically and religiously marginalised they were emotionally and personally caught up in the drama of their proclamation.

We see this intensity and integrity feeding one another and hurting inside the prophetic soul. Elijah, for example, fled to the desert, believing himself to be alone in Israel. The depression in his mind after the exaltation of the triumph over the prophets of Baal was deep and melancholic (1 Kings 19:4ff.). In Hosea the intense hurt of the truth broke through in one who knew and had experienced deep love and its appalling ambiguities (ch. 11). In Jeremiah we find the suicidal mood of the isolated single person whose message was such anathama to the leaders of the people and yet so profoundly true in his own perception (ch. 20).

The prophetic word involves conflict within and without the soul of the prophet. There is no cheap and easy word of prophecy in the Bible. The realities are so deep that they drive the prophet to question the heart of faith and the integrity of his or her own life. Can it really be as bad as it seems? The mark of the person of truth is a willingness to face it in all its hardness and difficulty.

False prophets tamper with the truth because they cannot face its consequences. They tell what people want to hear or more accurately what those who hold power want to hear. Societies captivated by false prophets allow themselves to be because the truth is too hard to bear and requires such radical change that it becomes far too disturbing. Let us rather get for ourselves prophets who will tell us what we want to hear. The starkness of this choice is seen in societies facing radical crisis in their conscience. Who told the truth in South Africa? Who avoided it? Who told the truth in the face of the Nazi terror and who avoided it? Who is telling the truth in the Holy Land today and who is avoiding it? Who is telling the truth about our Western values and their destructive power and who is avoiding it? Who is uncovering the character of our faith or its lack and who is avoiding facing this out?

The problem of the twentieth century is similar to that of Old Testament times – the Church is caught up in the collusion of the community in refusing the truth. The classic example of this is the failure of much of the Church in the face of Fascism in Europe at the heart of this century. In not too dissimilar manner some of the crucial Churches in the Afrikaner communities in South Africa could not face the truth but colluded with, and even provided justification for, the apartheid heresy. Who is having the courage to unfold the truth about the corrupting and debilitating effect of the selfish and individualistic materialism of post-Christian Western society and the collusion of the Church with it?

It will not do simply to look to the Church to be the prophetic voice who tells the truth. Church as the answer is going to be disappointing. The truth comes from beyond us. In the Old Testament it is the word from God. It comes from outside the immediate condition of the people. It is addressed to them. The prophets are those who hear the voice of God and, even against their own desires and sensibilities, proclaim it because they are convinced by it.

In an age in which the articulation of religious faith has proved troublesome to many we must not conclude that there is no word of truth for us to heed. It is possible that the truth has been given to us from the fringes of our culture and from sources which sit at a distance from traditional faith. God is not restricted nor is God partial. Truth remains truth whoever proclaims it. In the twentieth century, in an increasingly secular culture, we must be open to the idea that truth is addressed to us by those who are responding to the meaning and shape of our humanity in these times.

That is not to say that there must be some romantic baptism of art in the twentieth century. The artistic community, like the Church, struggles with questions of integrity. Art which speaks and endures, like theology, has to come to terms with the demands of the issues of truth. Art that avoids the difficulties and colludes with our capacity to evade the unpleasant and unpalatable nature of the truth about our living is, like theology of a similar ilk, superficial and will blow away with the changing winds of history. The artistic establishment can be as woeful as any other in colluding with the injustices of the present order. Truth often comes from those working on the borders of art.

God is not bound and those who listen for the truth must be ready to listen to unlikely and unexpected voices. The God who is both the creator and redeemer of all things may address us from many places. The crucial task for theology is to interpret what is being seen and heard. Contemporary prophecy needs its interpreters if it is not only to be heard but to be understood. The word is in vain unless there is interpretation. Without understanding the opportunity given by the truth for change may be lost. In the difficult but vital task of interpretation theology and art might connect with each other.

So theology should always be listening and watching. Listening to the endeavours of those who move on the edges of our culture and watching what is happening in their work. The theological task, if it is to impact upon our culture, must be done from within a sense of belonging to this society and this part of history. It cannot and must not be confined to the ecclesiastical world. It must be rooted in the totality of our human endeavour.

Prophetic voices in our own century

Pablo Picasso

To be confronted with Picasso's paintings is to be confronted with a critical part of the human story in our time. This is where we have come from. At the end of the nineteenth century the Impressionists had challenged the positivism of their time and broken open a new way of expression – painting that which is gained through the impression of the eye. The formalism and carefully structured art of previous generations gave way to a freer and more immediate art. Although much of it was concerned with nature and the impression on the eye and the mind of the painter, this new movement could not escape the searching questions concerning the structure of reality. Cézanne, in particular, sought through the medium of painting, to expose something of the structure of reality. He was concerned to reveal the understanding as well as the impression.

Picasso is the leading artist of the twentieth century who took this journey forward and shaped, thereby, the art of our time. It was Cézanne who influenced his early development. His paintings moved step by step in new directions. His link with Cézanne was not so much with the style of Impressionism but with the search for structure and meaning. Through the early years of Cubism, in a platonic sort of way, he seems to be searching for the universal behind the particular. Form and shape were the means of exploring the structure behind the immediate. His use of African images alongside classical ones gave a sense of primitive power and of mystical reality. The concern for the universal through the Cubist form gave an almost impersonal understanding of the human reality. If there is a strong sense of shape and of mystery in these paintings there is also a distance and even coldness about the human. Nevertheless, these human images have great power.[1]

Picasso's greatness, however, is in his refusal to stop on the journey. Before the tragedies of the Great War and of Fascism had afflicted our age, his thinking and painting had moved on to themes which might stand against the century yet to unfold. He came to see that the search for the absolute and for the universal was forlorn – love had been lost with the loss of the personal. He accepted that there are no universal realities behind the immediate. He opens the door to the possibility that the world we live in has no meaning. It has to be received as it is. We laugh or cry according to our own sense of relationship to it. He began to play with the forms in his paintings and introduced real things back into the pictures. There was a greater freedom and play in his work. There was also the sense of tragedy and even of the absurd which was to rise to the surface in Sartre's and Camus' writings soon after.[2]

Picasso's art confronts us with the dilemma of twentieth-century humanity – human beings who are close to being machines and whose life and culture speak of a humanity which is dead. Humanity is dead. When the tragedy of twentieth-century human life surfaces in the paintings, as for example in the famous 'Guernica' on the Spanish Civil War, what is Picasso protesting about? Is it a pro-communist and anti-fascist statement? Is it a protest again all violence and the appalling violence already experienced in the twentieth century? Is it an expression of the futility of human life as seen in this civil war? The painting, like all great art, leaves the viewer wondering and then thinking about the worlds we inhabit.

The extraordinary thing about Picasso, who stands like a giant over the art of our century, is that the essential steps in his work had been taken before the tragedy of the twentieth century became evident. He dared to raise the question as to whether you could have a sense of the universal without losing the human or of the absolute and still make sense of reality long before our century experienced the bloodbath of the First War and the brutality and mindless violence of both the Nazi terror and the Stalinist horror. To these terrible events must be added the appalling threat of the nuclear holocaust which hovered over us so closely in the years of the Cold War. The demand for universal solutions in the first half of the twentieth century crushed the human and threatened to destroy the delights of our diverse reality. Nature, God and humanity and even the world as we knew it all seemed to be threatened with destruction.

Picasso is the supreme prophet of the modern in the twentieth-century world of art. The threat that this project might end up in absurdity should, in no way, detract from its profundity. His work is large enough to speak in an emerging postmodern age because it exposes the character of modernity as we have experienced it.

Francis Bacon

If Picasso's paintings say something important about the condition of our twentieth-century culture, Francis Bacon's work is haunting in its message about the state of the human mind. At the heart of his work is a series of pictures which are comments on the famous Velázquez's portrait of the Pope Innocent X. Bacon's images are deeply disturbing. There is an existential pain and emptiness in them. The faces in the portraits are anguished, full of despair and yearning for a freedom which they cannot have. People are caged animal-like and in a deep and incurable angst. Bacon does not compromise in his painting of people in such a state of existential pain. The paintings offer no hope.

Who would not say that there is a great deal of hurt and confusion in the human soul in our time? The confidence in establishing sure relationships, understanding who we are and the nature of the possibility of our life, realising our place in the world and ensuring a constructive contribution to its welfare – these are elusive goods for people today. Anxiety, stress, a sense of being held captive to the tedium of our lives, inner uncertainty born of a distaste for the destructive certainties of others, and a yearning for a freedom most will not experience – are not these the truthful marks of so much contemporary life? We fear death, we seek a multitude of therapies and cures for our sicknesses of body, mind and soul. Is it not the case that the individual person is adrift in a world without purpose and living under the threat that it may have no real meaning? Bacon won't let us off the hook.

Only the courageous explorers of truth are willing to enter such dangerous territory. Bacon is among those who do so. The understanding of these things cannot be by way of denial but as response. We have to face the terror of our humanity if there is to be hope of glory.

The problem of our culture is that it has neither faced the terror nor the depth of its confusion and disaster.

The modern novelist

The truth can, similarly, be told by way of story. It was a favourite way in the teaching of Jesus. He told stories which uncovered the true character of the situation people were in – if they had ears to hear. Again, the prophetic task understanding our time and interpreting it so that we can find a way forward cannot avoid the difficult stories told by those who have written in this century. As with those who heard in Jesus' day so in our own time religious institutions have found it difficult to hear. We have fulminated against the sexual freedom of D.H. Lawrence and supported those who sought to censure his works. Others have issued fatwas against Salman Rushdie for his 'blasphemy' against the holy Prophet.[3] Focusing on the form of the story and on its outward challenge of orthodox morality or theology we have been deaf to the challenge such writing brings to our culture today. The complexities, hypocrisies and confusions of sexuality in the twentieth century are not caused by the modern novel. Our experience is their subject. Similarly the dangers of an over-serious attitude to orthodoxy and its potential threat to our human flourishing leads to the modern jester quietly but effectively using humour to tell us an important story. The Pharisees and leaders of the people shifted uncomfortably when Jesus told his stories. They heard them directed at them. So they were and directed at all of us when we are tempted into self-righteous mode. Whether we find them comfortable or not Lawrence and Rushdie write with beauty, power, insight and wit. Something of their own inner struggle is invested in the work. A measure of truth is to be found here and we know it. That is why we react so violently to what they say.

Camus

Who can read Camus' *La Peste*[4] and not be driven to the limits by its powerful existential and atheistic moral protest against the trite response of religion to the great plague of the 1930s and 40s which threatened to devastate the whole of European civilisation. Are we not all present in the church hearing the denunciations of the priest against the irreligion of the town – a piece of theological fascism which threatened to bind an already devastated and fearful people in its grip? Are we not all atheists as we leave that church in the night air of a town living with the plague?

Like Job in the Old Testament Camus resists orthodox approaches and insists we face evil in all its mystery and inexplicable injustice. Orthodox answers not only make no sense but are an affront to the reality being faced. Job all over again.

The twentieth century has been a century of unbelievable human suffering and most of it endured by those who are utterly powerless to resist – the innocent victims of forces and powers at work in our world which devastate the lives of ordinary people. Still the wretchedness persists – whole peoples driven from their homes and villages into permanent refugee status. Multitudes of the poor with the inevitable suffering and abuse inflicted on children, the sick, the old and the disabled.

Great plagues have racked our civilisation – the death dealing 'isms' of the twentieth century – Fascism, Racism, Leninism, Maoism, Capitalism, Fundamentalism . . . These terrifying universalising isms which demand our conformity. No wonder we live in a postmodern world afraid of universal truth and of absolutes. Small wonder we have retreated into the safety of a multitude of diverse and self-chosen cultures. When civilisation begins to destroy its own people then it is better to make for the hills and find safety elsewhere. Maybe in the safety of the hills people can dream again of freedom and truth and peace and community.

Music

Sometimes the level of terror launched on innocent people is so great that only the most subtle and profound of prophetic words will convey the depth of what is happening. The artists of the Soviet Union in Stalin's time must rank among the great prophets of our century. Endless purges of artists and peoples led to the most appalling destruction. Millions went to their death and millions more to the Gulag. It was in the midst of such horror that Dmitry Shostakovich composed his music.[5] During the appalling years of the 30s and 40s his symphonies spoke of the suffering of the people. After the war was over, although not himself a Jew, his use of Jewish music and song highlighted his moral commitment in the face of the Stalinist abuses. No musician in the twentieth century has spoken with such courage and power into the political world of his time. As a result he was purged and abused – denounced as a reactionary and as anti-Soviet. Shostakovich is a twentieth-century Jeremiah.

The capacity of music to speak to us in ways which are unique offers an important dimension to the artistic task. Dreams and hopes are kept alive within the human soul. We are helped to negotiate the outward awfulness by the journey inward which music invites us to take.

It is because of the work of those who continued to write stories and music even in times such as those of Stalin that hopes were kept alive for the future. What words sometimes cannot do music sometimes can. The story of the artistic community lives alongside that of the Church – similarly torn apart by the suffering. Compromised by the collusion and weakness of many of its leaders nevertheless in the hidden shape of the liturgy another story is alive and waiting for a different future.

Music and liturgy have the power to prevent the world being closed in around captive lives. Liturgy carries the worshipper towards the heavenly realities and towards the heart and meaning of love in freedom. Music, touching as it does, deep emotions within the heart can both protect the person and the community from the slaveries threatened without and help keep alive the flame of freedom and the possibility of love.

That is why those locked into the abuse of power find both religion and art a threat. True religion and courageous art are always a threat to tyranny. If we are to hear the voice of love in freedom we must listen for it on the borders of our culture and often among those despised by the powers of the day.

Who has told these truths? Not many and even fewer in the Churches. If, in the end, one of the great concerns of the Church as a community is living in the tradition which gave us the prophets and within which we came to know and love God in Jesus Christ, then in an age such as ours it needs the courage to search out and be with all who tread the hard and uncertain road of truth. The fact that many of those who have spoken with such power to the human condition in the twentieth century have often been far distant from the faith of the Church must not be allowed to prevent the growth of such a relationship.

If that is to happen the Church will have to be clear what it is and what it is not about. The abandonment of any project designed to promote 'Christian' art is inescapable. The idea that there is a superior sort of art coming from the Church only serves to deepen the divide. We start with a sense of shared humanity and with a common desire to discern the voice of truth as we reflect upon our human condition. Believing people share in the task and bring the dynamic of their convictions to it. They have no monopoly. The truth is beyond and to be discerned and discovered. It is not our possession even in the heart of the Church. Christians should know that. The truth is in Jesus – both encouraging us to believe it may reside within human life and history and reminding us that it is from God and not in our power.

A similar reticence about art which appears to be more sympathetic to the 'spiritual' will need to be part of our approach. The distinction between God and us – the Creator and the created – ought to enable us both to be cautious about the 'spiritual' worth of art and to be open to discern the nature of Being in all art. To invest spiritual power into works of art because of either their theme or their setting is to run the risk of idolatry. It is possible that we encounter more of the truth as it transforms our living in the Henry Moore sculpture in the park than in the religious statues in the church. Neither should be invested with properties which confuse their capacity to lead us to truth.

Resisting these temptations – creating a world of religious art – brings the question of truth in the arts out of the Church and into the artistic community itself. The common task of understanding and of seeing how we are being addressed by truth happens where the hard work is being done.

The Church has to be open to the possibility that the presence of God is to be discovered where many think God is absent and that God is absent where many think God is present. An understanding of reality which takes the freedom of the divine life seriously cannot evade that eventuality. The business of theological discovery is full of surprises. Truth, Being, the power of an eternal Love, the search for meaning, are not restricted to the places where traditionally they have been thought to be discovered. Sometimes even the language used about God confuses us. There is a sort of divine language – words about God which make God a subject of human study. The biblical language about God resists all notion of giving God a name or names. How can the source of all Being be named without reducing the divine to an idol under human control? The biblical language is the language of Being, of Love, of Truth, of Justice and Righteousness, of Peace. These eternal realities are other than us and yet may be found taking their life among us.

So God may well be discovered by any who are wrestling with the issues of truth and being, of love and meaning, of justice and peace. That those whose lives have been devoted by one vocation or another to their search cannot name the Name is not relevant to the question of where we discover the true nature of reality and so of God. The absent God who is here and the present God who is not here.

This has driven creative theology to the boundaries of our humanity. Why is Dietrich Bonhoeffer so powerful in the theological story of the twentieth century? Because he had the courage to make the full journey on the boundary of resistance to Hitler, even to the point of sharing in responsibility for the violence needed to seek to get rid of him. Bonhoeffer was willing to put himself outside the Church for the sake of the truth.[6] Was God, seen to be distant from the way of violence, absent or present in such extremis? Was the divine to be found in the Church which was confused to the point of compromise or near to the rebellious and violent conspiracy with which Bonhoeffer was associated?

Prophetic theology, like prophetic art, lives on the boundary and suffers for it. God, who is Being in Love, and Truth in Freedom, is discovered in the crucifixion of this in the encounter with the confusions, deaths and corruptions of our human condition.

The God who is Creator, Life-giver, Energiser, whose word opens up our human condition and whose paradoxical and symbolic presence is discovered in the changing cultures of our existence is the God who may be nearer than sometimes we dare to think on the boundaries of truth and meaning. The changing borders of art and culture may be a crucial place for such discovery in our own time. If we are to share the inhabitance of such a border we will have to recognise those who have worked there, often alone, throughout this past century. The courage, even of their unbelief, may be crucial to the shaping of what is still to come.

11

Media – the Virtual Reality of our Time

William Tyndale was the first person to translate the New Testament from its original Greek into English.[1] His success in communicating his work depended on the printing revolution of his day. The invention of the printing press tranformed communication in the early sixteenth century. Tyndale got his English New Testament to the people by using the most up-to-date printing technology. He had translated with a view to the lay person having the Bible in their own hands and in the everyday language of the people. He also wanted the people to hear the doctrines of the Reformation which he believed arose directly out of the Bible. Because of the opposition of many of the bishops, the Tyndale New Testament had to be printed in the Netherlands. Tyndale himself had to flee England for his own safety. The authorities eventually caught up with him and he was martyred. However, they did not succeed in destroying his work.[2]

Tyndale's story is a parable for our time. The then Bishop of London tried to destroy all copies of Tyndale's New Testament as they entered England. He bought them and he burnt them. But the bishop was fighting a losing battle. The printing presses were well able to keep pace with his bonfires. No sooner had he destroyed a batch than another arrived from the continent. Twenty years earlier the bishop would have won – the means for mass printing did not exist. The arrival of the printing press transformed communication. The establishment, in the form of the bishops, had difficulty coming to terms with it.

The twentieth century has seen an extraordinary revolution in communication. It is a change as significant as the invention of the printing press. Our century has witnessed the growth and diversification of the media. The people have access to an amazing and ever widening network of information and ideas. People now surf the Net and garner a wealth of information on a multitude of matters. A local action group, for example, can keep watch on a political situation in another part of the world via the Web. Up-to-date information is instantly available. What a transformation since the last century when it often took months for news to get to many parts of the world!

But let us return to the full story of the twentieth century revolution in forms of communication. In Victorian Britain the newspaper and broadsheet were the primary means of immediate communication. The development of the technology of printing allowed for mass production of news. A free press was considered essential for the protection of the public right to information. The printed newspaper was a reasonably cheap and effective way through which different interest groups and opinion holders could seek to win public support. The public demand for access to a free press lived then as now in tension with difficult questions about ownership and control.

Telecommunications and broadcasting

The invention of the telephone and of radio and television has changed the pattern of the way people and communities communicate and learn. The range and diversity of the world of newspapers can be contrasted with the early years of broadcasting. First the radio and then television were developed. In Britain they grew under a concept of Public Service Broadcasting. Set up in 1922 by Act of Parliament as a public body, but independent of Government, the BBC had a duty to provide a service to the public within the terms of its charter. Radio and television quickly established themselves as vital means for entertainment, culture, news and education. Religious worship and thought were included in the responsibilities of the BBC. At national and at local level the new broadcasting media became a critical part of the communication system of the nation.

Alongside these developments the telephone was beginning to bring first the national community and, secondly, the world into closer relationship. Together the telephone, the radio and then the TV ended the dependency of the world on written or personal communication for sharing news, opinion and information.

The post 1945 world has seen a mushrooming of these capacities. The growth of broadcasting, especially the spread of television, increased pressure for a diversification of opportunity in broadcasting. Independent broadcasters, such as the famous Radio Caroline moored off the coast of the UK, pressed for freedom to use the new media opportunities to give people choice and to enable independent bodies to use the networks. So independent broadcasting was born. The expectations, however, which the BBC had created through its balanced and high quality work influenced the establishment of independent broadcasting. The development of the independent sector in both radio and TV in Britain had to meet the demands of the standards of public broadcasting. Freedom of the networks did not mean a licence to broadcast without restraint.

Nevertheless the development of independent broadcasting increased choice and diversified the range of opportunity. At local and national level through both the BBC and the independent sector there has been a steady increase of choice. This diversification has raised a similar agenda to that posed by the press – who owns and controls the media and for what ends? Do these developments help or hinder in the promotion of freedom of information and opinion?

The satellite and IT revolution

If the development of the broadcasting media has been the first communications' revolution of the twentieth century IT and satellite has been the second. Satellite technology has made it possible to broadcast across the world – the world was made much smaller from a communications' perspective. Distance is no longer a barrier. Productions in the USA can be beamed via satellite into people's homes anywhere in the world. The satellite dish can be found in almost every community in the world. The development of space technology has not only changed our perception of the cosmos, it has made the whole world open to all its many parts. However fundamentalist the ayatollahs may have been in Iran, for example, they cannot shut that nation off from the impact of the satellite.

Then came IT – a revolution still happening as we write. A multitude of possibilities exist and continue to develop for communicating down the line. Digital technology had opened the way for fast systems of sharing information via the computer (the Web being the most obvious), the telephone system and the broadcasting media. The cable brings the phone system, the TV and the Net. Now the choice has multiplied. A host of specialist channels and communications opportunities are available to the person with cable or satellite.

Information and ideas can be shared from computer to computer allowing person-to-person communication. Anyone can put stuff on the net and anyone with the know-how can get it off. Again issues of freedom and control are raised by these developments.

Queen Victoria's funeral was watched by the millions who lined the streets of London. The primary means for reporting it to the rest of Britain and the world was the press. Princess Diana's funeral in 1997 was also watched by millions lining the streets of London. In addition thousands of millions were able to see it in full on their TV screens across the whole world. At one and the same time as the means of communication have diversified and broken free of the old systems of uniform public control they have united the world by enabling people everywhere to share events and ideas together. Yes, there are still places and people in the world without the resources and the means to take part. But even their world is being shaped by the ones undergoing this fundamental shift in communication systems. At one level there has been a breakdown of unity with the enormous diversification of the means of communication. At another the world has come together because contemporary systems enable fast and unfettered communication across the whole. We have become one world and we have become many worlds. There is no going back. Those not yet included will have to be brought in. Issues of equality of access and opportunity take on a new meaning in the face of these developments.

We should try to avoid the mistake made by the Church when confronted with William Tyndale's printed English New Testament. We cannot respond to the challenges posed by the contemporary world with the techniques of a previous order. Diversity and choice are here to stay. The world-wide immediacy is here to stay. It will be no good burying our heads in the sand by hoping that it will be possible to impose a uniform and centralised system of public order on all of this. All forms of the media have become a market-place. The interests of the people may better be served by attending to the nature and quality of the market than by regret at the sudden and explosive range of choice which people have in front of them.

It is, however, a very special sort of market. This market has power over opinion and plays a critical role in the shaping of the public agenda. There is, therefore, a major public interest in its quality. That interest in quality extends far beyond the immediate issues of how families are protected from, for example, access to child pornography on the Net. It concerns how ideas are presented, individuals and agencies protected from intrusion, how people are kept free of manipulative political and religious broadcasting. It concerns who chooses the agenda and how the power of ownership and control affects balance in what people have access to.

Choosing gives new responsibilities

– *eliminating monopolies*

There are a number of ways in which it is possible to guard the choices of the consumer. In a world where there are many possibilities for providing the service it is essential that power over it is disseminated. The principle which sought to under-gird public service broadcasting – that it is a coherent and united service to the public with proper systems of account-ability – now needs extending into the modern context. If there is to be a direct relationship between the provider and the consumer then accountability depends on the consumer being protected from private monopolies. The issue of choice has to be driven right back to who owns the media. Too many newspapers in the hands of one owner, too many channels under the control of one corporation, too large a slice of the IT market under one person's control, is bad for account-ability through real choice. Monopolies also threaten freedom and the responsibility of citizenship placed upon each person which depends upon people having open and balanced access to all public expressions of opinion.

That means that at the level of ownership there has to be independent control lest monopolies become dominant. It cannot be achieved by the unfettered operations of the market nor by a process of self-regulation. The public interest in diversity has to be protected by publicly established and enforced control over monopolies.

– *professional self-regulation*

A much more complex set of issues arises at a second level which concerns the inner dynamic of the professionalism of those who produce material and make it available. The easy route out is to lay the whole responsibility upon the people who have to choose. There should be total freedom for the media. It is for the public to decide what it will buy on the news stand, listen to on the radio, watch on the TV or access on the Net. At a very minimum level, however, the issue is not as simple. The newspaper bought on the way to work comes home in the afternoon and the children can pick it up. Children have easy access to both the radio and TV and increasingly skilled access to the Net. In any case you buy the paper for its headline or an aspect of its service and you have to take the rest whether you like it or not. In a decent and democratic society it is not unreasonable of people to expect some protection from undue exposure to violence, abuse of people and to corruption. Similarly, sections of our pluralistic community have a reasonable expectation that they will not be subjected to abuse in public. The media are clearly in the public forum. Black people and communities should not be abused by racist attack in the media, and the same applies to women and other sections of humanity who might easily be open to abuse if there were no restraints. There are boundaries to freedom which are there to protect all members of the community. The media are part of, not separate from, the society in which they fulfil their work. The essential freedom and independence by which they form part of the way the public are protected from the abuses of power cannot be read as putting them outside the borders of the shared values upon which the health of the community depends.

The confidence of the public depends on getting this balance right. There are two major threats to this contract between the media and the public. The first is the temptation of the state to want to use the media for its own partial ends. The media become an arm of the all-embracing state. A warning sign of oppression is first the desire and then the practice of government controlling the media. We have seen plenty of examples of that both in fascist and in Marxist societies in the twentieth century. Even in democratic societies too much external regulation can threaten the sharp edge of the way the media protect the public from abuse by corporate state power.

Yet the fact of the power of the media, witnessed to by the way oppressors like to control and emasculate it, leads to a recognition of the importance of all branches of the media exercising their power responsibly. The second danger, therefore, is failure by the media to ensure professionalism in these matters. Those involved in the media can all too easily get carried away and fail to recognise the enormous power in their hands; they forget such power can be abused and that people and agencies have real difficulty protecting themselves from the abuse which results.

If the first temptation leads to a move to free the media from any restraint, the second encourages the intrusion of the law and of the state into an area where freedom and independence are critical.

That would seem to suggest that self-regulation is important to public confidence and to the continued healthy contract between the public and the media. Self-regulation requires a clear acceptance of professional values appropriate to the various arms of the media. The multi-faceted world of today's communication systems requires a much stronger sense of professionalism within the media. The days are gone when broadcasters, for example, can rely on the Public Service Provisions to offer the protection needed. What was once delivered through a uniform system now has to be agreed and delivered by the profession itself. This is a further example of the way diversification places new responsibilities for agreed values and professional conduct upon the people directly involved. Judgements have to be made, monitored and regularly updated.

Effective self-regulation requires open and strong internal order and a system of independent monitoring. It also requires an effective system by which the public can call the profession to account. Just refusing to purchase the paper or watch the broadcast is not enough. Complaints have to be dealt with and the values and procedures agreed by self-regulation seen to be upheld.

One of the crucial issues concerns how real choice is protected and balance maintained. We have had a variety of experience in this. Choice and balance are maintained in the press both by a range of style of newspaper – from the broadsheet through to the tabloid, from national productions to very localised newspapers – and by a range of view and outlook. We expect papers to offer a diversity of political and social outlooks and all of them to exercise independence from whatever position they come. The broadcasting media have had a different experience. On radio there has been a variety of styles but all have to be seen to be balanced and independent on the expression of political, social or religious opinion. In TV the arrival of satellite and cable opportunities is moving this media from just having channels presenting balanced programmes within a distinctive stylistic commitment to one in which choice is achieved by the variety offered on different channels. If you want a film or sport or news or travel you turn to the channel that offers that service. Choice is enhanced by giving the people a greater range of options. Balance is achieved by ensuring that there is a sufficient variety of opportunities to meet a variety of public demands and needs.

In such a diverse world self-regulation which creates a culture of professional ethics and values is the only effective way of encouraging responsible work.

– the People have to accept responsibility as well

Choice involves us! At the third level we the people have to accept the responsibility which choice places upon us. The days when that duty could be safely left to the one public broadcasting network have long since gone. The issue which has always been with us in the press confronts us at all levels of communication today. We have to make real choices. That is what it means to live in this postmodern world.

The culture, however, has encouraged an attitude of passivity. We soak up what is offered to us. There is little sense of moral responsibility in us when we are responding to the media. We are given what we deserve and often what we desire. There has been virtually no serious discussion of what the expectation should be of us the media consumers. There has been plenty of discussion about what is expected of the media – little of what is expected of us who read, listen, watch and surf.

The level of Church contributions to this matter has not gone much further than campaigns to keep sex and violence off the screen and out of the papers, together with a regular defence of religious broadcasting. Look at the depressing level of Church resolutions on the subject. We just have not begun! We have not thought through the way we might develop values and habits which themselves will contribute to the excellence and professionalism of this new age of multi-dimensional communication.

We all of us spend a considerable amount of time watching TV, listening to the radio, in front of the computer and reading newspapers and magazines. That is not reflected in our educational programmes. What is done in home and school and church to help individuals develop their own critical faculties which, in turn, enable personal development and lead on to changing expectations of the media producers? We help people with how to manage their physical diet and to care for their bodies but what about the mind and soul, the imagination and the sources of creativity when in front of a TV or computer screen? Maybe there are media equivalents of a persistent diet of burgers and chips! Because the choice has increased so considerably it has become the more important that attention is given to helping one another with skills in making those choices.

Media studies should be an integral part of education. The aim is to create intelligent and morally alert consumers and choosers in a world in which media play such a vital role in a free society. The task is not to create an elitist attitude –

'broadsheet newspapers are better than the tabloids' – but to enable critical reflection and the dialogue of people's values with the different styles and means of modern communication. Discernment is what we need.

These developments enable both individual and group responses. It helps when different cultures and social groupings bring to the surface what they identify with or find good or recognise as properly challenging or enjoy as good entertainment. So the faculties which help people not only receive but respond to what is offered are strengthened. That strengthening leads to a response in the provider. This task of developing the skills of the consumer is about much more than having increasingly sophisticated market surveys. It is about deepening the freedom of people to make real choices.

Enabling people to make choices recognises and provides for the real relationship that exists between the public and the media. It will help to steer us away from that unhelpful passing on of responsibility which we saw something of in the public debate about the media at the time of the death of Diana, Princess of Wales. Should we blame the paparazzi, or the newspapers themselves that paid large sums for the photos, or the public who seemed to have an insatiable appetite for as much of the gossip as they could get? The strong relationship between the public and the media means that there must be a sense of common responsibility. Yes, the media have to look to their own professional ethical standards of conduct but the public need to reflect on what it is right to expect from the media. The choice lays responsibility on all. In this multi-media and multi-cultured age we have not attended enough to equipping people to contribute more maturely and creatively to this relationship.

Giving people the skills by giving time to critical reflection is likely to mean greater mobility by the public in the way they make use of the media. People may switch channel or switch off, change their newspaper habits and develop discerning skills in making use of the Net.

Choice has many good features to it. It recognises that human need varies from group to group and at different stages of life. It meets the demands of a community made up of people of different needs and cultures. We should not regret it but make positive use of it.

Religion in the media

All the media have to make sense of what to do with religious questions. The Church frequently reduces the issue to one concerning religious broadcasting but, in a similar way to the debate about the place of religion in education, it is rather a case study in the way we interpret freedom today.

The recognition of the part religious belief plays in the lives of individuals and communities means that we need to think about how this dimension is handled across the range of media life. How are people's beliefs and the religious institutions they belong to presented in the media? Is there a fair and adequate reporting of religious matters? We need to distinguish between an honest presentation of how people view religion and religious bodies and a dispassionate concern for truth and the way believers understand that for themselves. Humour can sometimes help us make that distinction as we learn to laugh at our own stereotypes and even prejudices.

Religious institutions may well need to be both tougher and more professional in the way they respond to how they are represented (or not). Why were these events reported and not those? Why are we so frequently stereotyped in these ways? An honest and open engagement with the media can be mutually beneficial. A tough conversation only makes sense when it is clear that the Church appreciates the media world and task. Such a relationship might help us learn how we are perceived rather than how we would like to be perceived. Media people get a more truthful understanding of what we believe and why. Professionalism all round is improved. Sometimes that conversation can move to a deeper level of thinking through the basic values and ideas which the media are putting about. It is important to know how well these relate to the values and ideas which are rooted in faith. So the conversation needs to go beyond just the quality of 'religious' broadcasting.

The explosion of possibilities in the media has opened the door to specifically religious channels. The USA has long known religious broadcasting paid for by subscription. That is the counterbalance which preserves freedom in a constitution which keeps a rigorous divide between the state and religion. British constitutional history is different and we need to interpret the way freedom works within our own tradition of political and public life. That is why moves in Britain to open up the channels for 'Christian' radio or TV cannot simply be justified on the American model. Alongside the idea of specific religious channels independent producers can offer their work to the mainstream broadcasting companies. That opens the door to some imaginative contributions which have to meet the rigorous demands of excellence in broadcasting.

All media have to meet the agreed professional standards set for everyone – the outcome of self-regulation and obligations placed on all people by the law in a democratic society. If we are to have specifically religious channels – and the argument has to be made within our culture – then a number of things need to agreed.

First, we must reject any suggestion that the religious channels are the 'Christian' ones and the rest are secular. The creation of a hierarchy of value based on the provenance of the channel is not sound in terms of our faith. A religious label does not guarantee either good media work or even truthful media work. We might judge, on the basis of our beliefs, that the 'secular' media are better than the religious ones!

Second, there must be a commitment to excellence in standards of production. The highest professionalism should mark out all religious broadcasting. Religion cannot be used as a protector of the second-rate. The Churches have a lot of catching up to do to demonstrate an understanding of excellence in professional life.

Third, there must be fairness and responsibility in the representation of people's views. Religious groups are prey to stereotyping those they don't agree with. Good media work allows people to speak for themselves before offering comment and perspective on their view. Where are the independent structures of accountability?

Fourth, if a newspaper or TV channel has a specific set of beliefs and values to which it is committed, it must be open and clear where it is coming from. I know when I read *The Guardian* newspaper that it comes from the liberal and radical end of the political spectrum and, by contrast, when I read *The Daily Telegraph* that it is on the right of democratic politics. But I expect them both to be clear about that and independent in ensuring a fair and balanced presentation of news. Principled religious broadcasting should have a similar commitment.

Finally, all exploitative methods of using the media to pressurise people in their responses should be avoided. Consumers must be given proper space to make their own judgement and response.

All of these values make good sense of religious belief in the heart of the historic religions of the world. Things which fall outside these boundaries are likely to be sectarian and tend to be unhelpfully divisive and destructive. Love working for freedom moves against sectarianism and towards inclusiveness. There is a subtle but important link with the Christian understanding of the heart of reality. This is where belief and practice interrelate.

The revolution in communications is not over. We will have to adjust ourselves continually to its changing possibilities. The future looks set to increase choice and enable diversity. For that to be good there will need to be some agreements about values and professional conduct. Like William Tyndale we must engage with the most up-to-date systems and what they offer if we are to continue to play a part in ensuring good and healthy outcomes.

Coming to terms with the meaning of postmodernism in the media age of the twenty-first century is critical for those who search for values which humanise and cohere an ever changing and multi-faceted world. The media are the open symbol of the basic challenge of our age.

Section IV

Church and Its Meaning
for Our Time

The Church avoids the challenge of the changing culture to its peril. If the bad news is that it will struggle with what is required and fret over it like every other institution bringing the past with it, the good news is that sharing in that struggle it might yet offer some hope to the whole human endeavour.

For that journey it will need the full riches of its inheritance of faith and the courage to allow the paradoxes of its faith to open the way for a new reformation of its understanding, its order and its sense of place in society.

That task cannot be predicted. It can only be faced and worked upon. Like any journey forward to a future as yet not fully revealed the surprises will be many, the difficulties at times seem insuperable, the confusions deepening, the joys and the pains constantly interacting. But this is the gateway to life. The other road of doing nothing and hoping the challenge will go away has death written all over it. Life, however, is what it is all about – and life enabling love and liberty!

12

The Church

The culture we inhabit presents the Church with a stark choice. It either gives in to the divisive tendencies of an empty postmodern world and collapses into congregationalism or even sectarianism, or it faces the risky and confusing challenge to work for communion across the diversity of our kaleidoscopic world. The delusion of the sectarian option is that one day it will conquer and the culture will submit to it. In the various millennialist versions of this the conquest happens at some apocalyptic point beyond the realities of ordinary history. The Churches in the United Kingdom, if not in other parts of the Western world, are in immanent danger of drifting into a close-knit congregationalism. In some cases on the extremes of Church life this is close to becoming sectarianism. If the Churches view the community, outside the bounds of their immediate congregation, as hostile or at best neutral, the temptation is to establish a clear boundary between the two. You are either in or you are out. In effect that means most people are out.

The gospel edge

The Christian gospel has a sharp edge. It involves radical conversion. The reality and, indeed, necessity for the new birth is an inescapable part of the Christian tradition. Entry into Christ's new Kingdom means being committed to a fundamental change of heart and with it a new and different direction in life. Jesus called people to enter the Kingdom of God, to repent and to believe in the Good News (Mark 1:15). Baptism into Christ is the sign of this turning round and

179

beginning again. So a person becomes a member of a community making this journey together.

The assumption that radical conversion leads to a life apart from the world we inhabit needs overturning. The radicalism of the Kingdom is about new horizons, freedom to grow and explore the journey of faith and the creation of a community which includes rather than excludes. It demands an opening up of the life of the Church so that all people and communities may the more easily and critically encounter the Good News which promises so fundamental a change in human lives and societies. We forget that the gospel is Good News. Sectarianism is invariably bad news for people.

The Church, treating its sacraments and catechumenate with great seriousness and discipline, is not at all led from that to a closed world of cosy ecclesiastical life – whether that takes a Catholic, Evangelical, Charismatic or any other form in the Christian tradition. The demand of the gospel increases freedom and widens love.

At its centre the Church is defined by the vision of God offered to the world in Jesus Christ. It is a community travelling that risky but revolutionary journey of faith and hope in Christ. On the boundary, however, of its relationship with the wider world it will be open and moving. So it will not be at all easy to draw the line of the border with any sense of precision. Sharing in the community of the gospel is not like crossing a frontier where suspicious officials check that the passports and visas are in order. The frontier is free, unseen and runs through the middle of our lives and communities and cultures. The New Testament image is of wheat and tares growing together until harvest. In such a world weeding is a dangerous pursuit! The message is, stop trying to purify the Church. Leave the sorting out to God.

The Church is always and for ever seeking ways of enabling those caught by the vision to continue their life in the whole community. In reverse it is called to help those whose lives are rooted in the world to catch a sight of the vision of God. The Church cannot, therefore, afford the sort of border mentality which requires all who enter (or leave!) to produce their ecclesiastical passport and to live under the constant threat of being frisked of any sign of 'worldliness' as they pass through customs. Neither should it encourage its members to view the world out there as hostile country only to be risked on occasion and that when fully armed! Rather we should expect a continual flow of people in and out of the worshipping community. In a postmodern world the less clear we are about the membership of the Church the more likely it is to be living in the Good News.

There are many different images which offer different aspects of the meaning of Church. In recent years we may have given too much emphasis on the corporate fellowship of the Church and too little on its common life being shaped by a shared hearing of the Word of the gospel. The former runs the risk of locating the Churches' unity and form in the common life of the people, the latter in the vision and the journey. The stress moves from the inward conversation about the quality of people's faith and of the ensuing fellowship towards a concern for the presentation of the truth of the gospel in Word and sacrament. So the Church is present where the gospel is made visible and people come to witness and respond. This means that the Church is always open to any who, for whatever purpose, join together to hear the gospel Word. Article 19 of the Thirty-Nine Articles claims: 'The visible Church of Christ is a congregation of faithful men, in which the Word of God is preached, and the sacraments be duly administered . . .'[1] By emphasising the visible Church as a gathering of people where Word and sacrament are central, the Prayer Book gives it a sense of life and mobility. It is not all that easy to draw the borders of such a Church. It is a definition which can be made more inclusive. The emphasis moves away from the authenticity of the rites of initiation to the gospel mystery which will never be wholly contained by such forms. So the Church becomes the community of the baptised and a lot of hangers on as well! Hazy boundaries which draw us to the paradox and mystery of the love of God.

This image can certainly be built upon as it focuses on the Good News made visible in Word and sacrament defining the Church. If both Word and sacrament have an all-life embracing quality they include the journey people travel to make the gospel visible in life and action in society. There is movement as people travel inwardly and outwardly in the life of faith.

The eternal fire

The vision of God revealed to us in the gospel of Christ is like a perpetual blazing fire which draws individuals and communities towards it. Every year at the season of Bonfire Night in November the London Borough of Islington holds a massive public bonfire and firework party. On a good night 60,000 people can be there. The bonfire party is a great image of the Church as it is called to be today. Watch the company of people gathered round the fire. They are some-what untidily assembled. Some will feel the need to be close in near the blaze, others stand further off watching and wondering, and even further away are those conscious of the fire but not yet wholly attentive to it. All the time some are drawing near and others moving away. The fire itself seems to encourage the movement. There are people on their own drawn to the warmth, family groups and small communities there. The thing which unites all is not necessarily their mutual knowledge of each other but the power of the blaze at the heart of what is happening.

The Good News is a fire burning at the heart of the community. The fire burns on and works its purpose in good times and in bad shaping the lives of those drawn within its orbit. Large and small crowds come and go towards it and away from it. Different sorts of communities and cultures are drawn to its powerful warmth and living power. It is a mystery creating community without destroying what people bring in themselves to it.

The Church's strategy

In an age of pluralism of faith and of widespread unbelief what might this mean for Church strategy? The Church has tried a number of ways of opening itself up to the wider community. Some congregations have gone down the road of popularising the core faith of the Church in their worshipping and teaching ministry. Simple services in easy language with popular styles of presentation have been widely used in recent times especially but not exclusively in Evangelical and Charismatic Churches.

Another way has been one by which the events and life of the community have been brought into church. Church buildings in areas of deep social need have become community centres, vibrant with social activity and service to needy localities. Those committed to a social vision of the gospel have chosen this road of linking into the wider world.

These two approaches, though in some crucial ways contrasting in theology, have some things in common. They both struggle with the dilemma of the distance between the tradition of the Church and contemporary culture. They are both concerned to build bridges. They are evidence of the determination of Christians to make connections. They are, at least, seeking to make some sense of the gospel in a diverse and bewildering culture. If we are to respond to the integrity of their search we need to stand back and take a critical look at what we are doing through these models of Church life. There is a danger of these approaches becoming reductionist solutions to a properly perceived problem.

The Charismatic search for easy common worship and faith could collapse into a minimalist and reductionist creed. The mystery and openness of truth is lost in simplistic credal demands. It hopes a concentration on fundamentals will help get people to cross the bridge. In that there is some success.

183

But then there is real difficulty moving on. Words cannot move on to truth.

The other tries to find a common ground in the essential works of love and service which are themselves sacraments in the secular order. Since it is difficult to talk directly and meaningfully about the faith with people it is thought that people may catch it obliquely from the integrity of the Church in its life of service. Again, it is difficult to move on and enable people to articulate, for themselves, the meaning of the vision. The loving service is vibrant and free but the connection with the mystery of truth is difficult to articulate. Action finds it difficult to root itself in being.

This is the intellectual and cultural dilemma to which the Sea of Faith Movement is responding.[2] Here the creative experience of faith substitutes for the reality of ontological truth. Spiritual experience substitutes for God. It is assumed that the form in which Christianity has come down to us through the ages is no longer believable. Outdated structures of thought through which the gospel has been mediated to us must be left behind. In this case it is the whole intellectual credal shape of the faith which is no longer believable. If we cannot have the faith we can have the benefits.

All of these responses – different and contradictory though they are in many ways – are reducing the core to what is thought to be essential. What is considered essential is different in each case – simple credal assertions rooted in easy worship, dedicated action for the diverse needs of a vulnerable society or the essential experience of faith as opposed to the substance of belief. What is common is the analysis and process which lets go what is seen to be unessential.

Moving on from reductionism

A reductionist strategy of whatever sort is doomed to fail. It is the full vision we need if our humanity and our society are to be brought to life once again and if we are to make something of the many faces of our contemporary living.

Must we, however, move down the road of reductionism at all? Does the existence of the gulf between our secularised culture and the world of faith require it? The recovery and renewal of the spiritual and moral foundations of our social order lead to a different strategy – one rooted in confidence that the well-being and good of the community and its culture will be enhanced by a wider and fuller vision. Our task is nothing less than to enable more and more circles of our living to appreciate the mystery, sacredness, holiness, glory and beauty of the spiritual realities which undergird all decent and good human experience. A reductionist strategy – however good its intentions – has no hope of arriving at this destination.

Worship as a key to the future

If it is a sense of mystery, beauty and wonder which provide the spiritual resources whereby we can learn to live decently and imaginatively in the varying circumstances of modern life, then worship is likely to have a critical role in getting us there. If worship is the medium through which individuals and communities explore the interplay between the being of God and their own being – a link between the spiritual and natural orders – it is pivotal to enabling us to reintegrate our lives and our social order.

Sadly, in our culture worship has been privatised and anaesthetised. Little thought has been given in the creation of public worship to the shape of life people are called to in the contemporary world. The dynamic between worship and service has been severely undermined. Church services have become a leisure time pursuit and primarily aimed at domestic life.

Recovery will need the worship of the Church to cease being understood as a private affair for believers conducted in the domestic setting during leisure time. Worse still it becomes a rather second-rate leisure time pursuit. Since so much domestic life has become privatised in the twentieth century and sometime even detached from the heartbeat of human relationships in their many faceted reality – it is not surprising that people have come to see religious worship as a private matter for those who choose it. On entering the church door people are all too often asked to abandon any sense of excellence and required to leave behind much of their day-to-day experience. The public nature of the event has been virtually lost.

When congregations of Christians offer their worship to God – however small their number may be – they are making an offering for all. In a sense every time Christians worship God they bring the rest of the community and the created order with them. In difficult times these small companies of worshippers keep alive the vision of God for all. The fire burns on even if not many are gathered close to it at this moment in history. The fire is there for all not just for those gathered near to it there and then.

This is a means through which the mystery of the liberating love of God transforms people's lives. The encounter with worship needs to be liberating. At present it often seems to demand an outmoded conformity which sits ill with the complexity and diversity of contemporary living. It is the Son who sets us free and we are, thereby, truly free. That freedom moves through the wonder of worship.

The way worship is shaped needs to reflect this. Worship has within it the four things missing from the grey secularism of our age. They are glory, community, love and holiness.

Glory

At its heart worship calls us close to the being of God and renews the vision of God in the midst of our created existence. The glory, the beauty and the mystery of the Divine should inhabit true worship. All should lead us from one realm of reality to another. There should be moments when those who encounter worship should feel themselves transported into the heavenly places – to the heart of God. The music, the art, the silence, the movement should have a transparency that is able to be used by the Spirit of God. It should be a foretaste of encountering God face to face. The outcome is the reviving of that sense of wonder and mystery within humanity which is so vital to the flourishing of all things good. It is this which creates a sense of humility and an understanding of the limits of our living.

This is an inner journey made by individuals and communities. It cannot be reduced to definition. Yet often people speak of experiences of this nature when they are caught up in worship. It is a moment of movement within the person and community where space is created for the world beyond us. So worship needs to happen. Our doing is entirely secondary to the mystery of God working from the divine being to the being of humanity and the world. Glory is about being. That requires space – inner space.

Community

The corporate nature of worship – the fire draws people together around it – is creative of community. Community is not created by like-minded people coming together to keep others out – the sectarian option. It is created when people who otherwise might be pulled apart are brought together. They are united, not by that which is in themselves, but by the sharing of vision and hopes and by the wider shared sense of the Divine. In our atomised disintegrating world, the Church, through worship, keeps alive the hope of inclusive and affirmative community. When we are in worship something greater calls us together. By one route or another the Church, when it has sought to be faithful to the vision of God which called it into existence, has always been a power keeping community alive in times of darkness and fragmentation.

That surely is the history of the role of the Church in South Africa these past generations. It was certainly the history of early monasticism at the time of the collapse of the Roman

Empire. It has been the contribution of the great revival movements such as Methodism during the terrible years of social disruption at the Industrial Revolution: the Church acting as a power for community through worship. The transforming effect of John Wesley's preaching and creation of Methodist order is a classic example. First the fire is seen and heard. Then the excluded are drawn in and formed into effective community. That vision eventually spilled out in parts of Britain in the building of the Labour Movement – from the Methodist Class system liberating working people through the articulation of faith to the Trade Union Branch and meeting. The consequence for those so affected has been a sense of belonging and inclusion. People who might otherwise have been left out in the cold have been brought into the warmth of the community of faith and of a democratic and more equitable society: the interplay of vision, faith, community and social development.[3]

This is difficult for the Church and always has been. The difficulty is in the fact that the essence of the community of the Church is in the differences between its members. Sameness is not a mark of a truly Christian Church. Difference is the mark. It is a signal of an ultimate unity which is the meaning of God for humanity. It is difficult because catching the vision and finding that the people who seem so different from you have caught the same vision means there is no avoiding having to make sense of this new community which overcomes the divisions of the old. The temptation is to try and make the Church safe from the divisions of our immediate communities – to make the Church into a cultural ghetto. A diverse and postmodern world will not be able to make any sense of such ghetto Church order. People of all opinions, all sorts of cultures and lifestyles are thrown together by the sharing of the journey made possible by the vision of God offered to all in Jesus Christ.

Such a gospel culture of inclusion and diversity in the Church is going in a very different direction from the conformist congregationalism and sectarianism of the drift of Western Church life today.

Love

The Being of God is eternal love. It is out of the eternity of love that the creation came to be and out of it has come the transforming and liberating life of salvation. A glimpse of God is a sight of love. The glory, the beauty and the mystery lead us to the meaning of all things in love. If humanity, starved of the power of love in community, stills longs to find something of its effects, the Church can open the way of love through the experience of worship. We have not encountered God if we have not sensed the challenge of a love greater than our own and different from even the best we have yet known. People flourish in the warm atmosphere of divine love. We grow, we learn, we prepare for new futures and we discover new visions for ourselves and our world.

Love is dangerous because it always threatens to change us and to demand our penitence. It is the opposite of the forces which try and keep us and the world as it is. Divine love moves us and the creation on towards the as yet unseen fullness of the purpose of God for all. The result of this is the energising of service and the creating of new vocations. Such energising begins to attack the despair, the disillusionment and the alienation of the secular world. The powerful forces of materialism which depend for their success on the weakness and inactivity of the alienated are undermined by the energising effect of love on the excluded.

The alternative characteristic of the Church is not in some separated culture but in its struggle to prevent the world excluding what God has included. Its service is always challenging the assumptions of the prevailing power structures of the time. It constantly points forward refusing to allow the world to stay where it is but encouraging it to move on by addressing the experience of the victims of the present. Social action is not a luxury on the edge of Church life but integral to its identity as a gospel institution.

Holiness

The encounter with God is a meeting with the holy – the One who is different from us and calls us forward to a new life and to new possibilities. If worship restores dignity to the broken it also gives a sense of place to everyone because in it we are reminded of the limits of our humanity and of our weakness, fragility and of our compromised conscience. It is the counterbalance to the brash humanity of the secular world which knows the answers and insists on its own way. In the face of the eternal holiness of God we discover our place and we learn both the necessity of penitence and the liberty of contentment. Neither penitence nor contentment are acceptable ideas in a self-confident secularism. Yet in a world torn apart by the violence we do to each other and the crippling effects of unrecognised guilt the rediscovery of forgiveness in public affairs would help to undo the wrongs of our own century. The Church must keep alive a sense of the holiness of eternity, of the accountability of all human life and of the sanctity of the created order.

The experience of forgiveness is the other side of the meaning of holiness and it has a powerful dynamic in the creation of community and of a different future for the world. Contrast the stories about forgiveness in the Gospels – the story of the tax collector restoring what he had misappropriated – with the difficulty if near impossibility of people involved in modern public life in being able to admit to failure and find the power to start afresh. No wonder both the media and the public find profit and entertainment in the weakness of those in public life. Public life is based on success. That is brash and destined to fail because failure and weakness are integral to the human condition. Forgiveness assures us that our limitations can be turned to advantage when we are prepared to accept the boundaries to our capacity to order and control our own destiny. Human achievement can only be founded on forgiveness and a sense of humility. Basing it on the self-justification of contemporary culture is self-destructive. We can do things well only when we know the limits. Let God be God and then there is freedom for humanity.

When we consider such themes and see how rich they are, not just for the immediate life of the Church, but potentially for all, we can begin to see how important it is that the Church resists the temptations of reductionist strategies, however well-meaning their origin might be. Nothing less than the full wonder of the mystery of God's self-revelation is needed for the broadening of our visions and the recovery of our humanity in these times.

Such strategies have a long-term perspective. The short-term gain may be useful but can be ephemeral. What we are about is nothing less than the long-term recovery of the spiritual dimension of human living and through it the renewal of our community and its culture. If previous decades have seen the steady erosion of these beliefs and values with the consequent destruction of so much that makes for open and wholesome social life, then the recovery is likely to take just as long. The Church has to learn both consistency and patience. Consistency in the vision that stirs it to life and patience to work with the timescale of the Kingdom of God. In the interplay of vision and a postmodern world the future is shaped.

Changing the Establishment for the Good of the Nation

Two principled desires live at best in tension and at worse in conflict in our own society. These are the desire to live in freedom and at peace with one another and the desire to secure a society rooted in Christian values. The way the latter is presented often seems to involve the imposition of unwanted values and norms upon minority groups. In our multi-faceted society the old privileges of establishment look increasingly like an imposition from the past. In the context of the experience of the twentieth century which has done so much damage to the inherited understanding of Christendom it becomes virtually impossible to justify. The question about the place the Church holds in such a social order is a micro-cosm of the issues faced by the whole establishment.

From a political point of view our future is dependent upon our ability to hold together a diverse and ever changing culture. The peace of the nation depends upon its capacity to include all its citizens in a sense of belonging and ownership. That is always a struggle. At the end of the twentieth century it is inescapable. Many different cultures form the nation. Policies of exclusion lead to conflict and even violence. There are occasions when the fundamental integrity of the nation is brought into question as parts of the community demonstrate their frustration and anger at persistent exclusion. The 1981 riots in Brixton and elsewhere were such an occasion. The anger of black people and communities at their exclusion through persistent discrimination called into question the integrity of the whole political community. It was recognition of that reality, as well as an element of fear, which drove government to a full and independent inquiry under Lord

Scarman.[1] We still journey with the issues raised in his report – issues which go deep into our culture and require a dedicated and unyielding movement for change.

Democracy and repression?

Societies live on a continuum between democratic life on the one end of the pendulum and repression on the other. The temptation of those who try and enforce unwanted norms of behaviour on different cultures is to think that a measure of enforced repression is the only effective way of holding a diverse society of conflicting interests and cultures together. The way of freedom and democracy seems so full of risk. Enforcing conformity has sometimes been seen as the only way of protecting the safety and integrity of the nation. A culture of conformity entered the soul of the nation in the sixteenth and seventeenth centuries. Since the battles of these centuries much of the legal framework of the establishment has been rooted in the attempt at enforced conformity. How else could a Protestant nation be kept free of the lurking papal threat? How could it be protected from those radical and dissenting forces which threatened the break up of its perceived identity? So we inherited a series of constitutional provisions and laws about holding on to the necessary conformity to our historic identity. The Repeal of the Test and Corporation Acts in 1828 began a crucial process of dismantling some of the excluding features of this conformist culture. Critical features of the establishment, however, remained intact.

This culture of the protection of our established forms of religious and political life provided plenty of ammunition for bitter political struggles throughout the nineteenth century and into the early twentieth century. In the Victorian era the established Church and dissent fought over education and the control of schools and of religious instruction, over the establishment here and in Ireland and Wales, and over the relationship of the Crown to the Church and its government.[2] They fought political battles over burials and marriages. At local and national level pro- and anti-establishment forces sought to gain control of power. In the parish where I served my title a fierce and bitter struggle had taken place over sixteen years after 1880 between the rector of the parish and the local elected and Nonconformist controlled Burial Board about the new burial ground. The rector wanted it consecrated and refused to bury people in unconsecrated ground. The Burial Board wanted it dedicated so that it was kept free of the privileges of the established Church. In the end, after years of bitter division, the new burial ground was divided in half – half of it was consecrated and half not. So Anglicans and Nonconformists could be buried according to their convictions! That was but one of a running series of battles between the establishment and those who wanted disestablishment. The Irish question (which has been the subject of another chapter) was another battleground between the advocates of establishment and dissent.

Education – a crucial test case

There have been three different but complimentary areas of debate and conflict in the handling of education in a plural society.

The radical option

In the Victorian era radical dissent proposed to take religion out of education altogether. The teaching of the faith belonged to the Church. Schools had no business engaging in this task. In areas such as Liverpool and the North-West of England this battle of ideas was keenly fought. There were large numbers of church schools and the region had real difficulties with religious pluralism. The rapid growth of the Irish Catholic population brought the religious divisions of Ireland on to English soil. The established Church responded to this challenge by building church schools. Here the true

Protestant faith could be secured to the next generation and the position of the established Church maintained. Schools were seen as part of the way the values and faith inherited from the past and represented in the establishment could be guarded for the future. Radical dissent, by contrast, responded in an entirely different way. They wanted the establishment dismantled and the state removed from any influence upon the Church. They carried the logic of their argument the whole way in looking to secularise schools. Teaching religion in schools meant the door remained open for the state to interfere in the teaching of the faith. Religion and education needed separating.

This is, of course, the model at work in the USA which observes a strict constitutional divide between Church and state. Public schools – those funded and run by the government – are not allowed any practice of religion nor its teaching in school. There are no acts of worship in these schools and no religious instruction. Such a position is seen to be essential to the democratic integrity of the constitution.

In the twentieth century, in Britain, the principled voice of radical dissent has been taken over by the non-religious forces of secular humanism. The voice calling for the end of religious observance in worship and the end of religious education in schools comes primarily from this agnostic/atheistic source. It is the sort of programme advocated by the British Humanist Society.

This is one way of dealing with the dilemma of pluralism in our society and of preventing minorities feeling themselves excluded. Those who do not have a religious faith or who belong to minority religious cultures would not have to remove their children from formal acts of worship or religious education. It is an attractive solution because of its simplicity. Divide Church and state. Leave the Church to teach the faith in freedom but keep all aspects of the state clear of any involvement in any formal religious activity. It is the rigorous disestablishment view.

The non-denominational approach

A second approach has been to take the sting out of the issue by ensuring a non-controversial approach. It was felt that the conflict had to be removed from the nineteenth-century denominational struggle in education, and so religious education and worship in state schools must be non-denominational in ethos. Much of the present practice derives from this history. Proselytising is banned in all schools. The content of religious education courses has to be agreed by representatives of the Churches and of the main faiths through SACRE Committees where the work done seeks to avoid partisanship. Collective worship is aimed at being inclusive and styled to the needs of each local community. Not that with successive Education Acts these matters are entirely free of controversy today. The last Conservative Government in Britain sought to enshrine in legislation the central role of the Christian religion. They maintained that this accurately reflected our history and culture, and that children needed to be taught the Christian religion and enabled to encounter basic Christian worship. Nevertheless the ethos worked out of the conflicts of the nineteenth century still holds and both religious education and worship in state schools are non-denominational and inclusive in style.

This is the essential compromise which ensured what most people wanted – the continued exposure of their children to worship and prayer and the teaching of the basic tenets of religious faith especially as they formed a basis for the development of moral life and the enabling of children to grow in personal values which would help in their future life in the community. The evidence of opinion gatherers is that the majority of people still look for such an outcome.

The compromise has made a diversity of experience possible. There are church schools which have a stronger Christian curriculum and a clear shape to their pattern of common worship. Such provision has enabled communities, such as the Roman Catholic community, to ensure that their own children have consistent teaching in church, home and school. State schools can be more wide-ranging and have no denominational commitments. They are, however, able to meet the widespread desire in the community to ensure that children and young people face up to the challenge of religious belief and to find their own place in response to the history and form of the culture of this society. From different starting points both church schools and state schools seek an inclusive way of handling both the content of education and the style of collective worship.

The problems are in a tendency to reductionism – only to focus on those parts of religion which are not as controversial as others. The temptation is to sink religious education and worship to the lowest common denominator approach. Religion is restricted to a sort of basic and non-controversial social and personal morality. The great issues of faith are avoided because schools and teachers are ill-equipped to handle them. Better to keep the lid on the difficult bits!

Multifaith communities and the question of justice

The third approach has been concerned with questions of justice and equity. The postwar concern with the development of our society into a multifaith community has brought this issue into sharp focus. We are no longer dealing with the problems of managing a multidenominational society or even a society in which many are sceptical of religion altogether. We are dealing with a society with significant and growing sections of its people who are of other faiths than the Christian faith. The presence of Jewish communities meant that the question was always present but it had not been faced with any rigour until the postwar process of immigration from the old empire brought large numbers of Muslim people, Hindu people and Sikh people to British cities and into this society. Church schools, which in the past had struggled with their role in city communities where so few had much to do with church, now had to provide for classes of children

90 per cent of whom were of other faiths. That posed a new challenge.

Recent legislation has tried to respond to this by seeking to preserve the central role of Christianity in religious education and worship. Education authorities and schools have the difficult task of providing good religious education and attractive acts of worship in a rapidly changing cultural context and one which affects different localities in radically different ways.

The principle of inclusiveness moves in the direction of ensuring fair and adequate treatment of all faiths. The principle of our historic Christian inheritance moves in the direction of ensuring that neither the roots nor the values of our inherited culture are lost in the process. Different communities have different needs. Nevertheless education which takes account of the multifaith society we now share in together needs to affect all communities and not just those with an immediate multi-cultural shape. These are difficult balances to strike. Creative work both in the content of school programmes and in enabling young people to encounter worship in an inclusive and challenging way allows understanding to grow and freedom to flourish in diversity.

The difficulties facing establishment

The danger of the tension between our inheritance and the realities of a society such as ours is that the inheritance will be seen as imposition – nearer the oppressive end of the pendulum than the end of freedom. Established religion is imposed and, therefore, in principle an enemy of the vision of a community living at peace in its freedom. Democracy and establishment are thereby set at odds with each other. There can be no defence of establishment if that is the ground of the debate.

We might, however, find some creative ways forward by getting behind the issue and seeking some shared ground. Establishment and the history of the divisions which go with it give the impression that Christian faith and the institutions of Christian religion involve a uniformity which sits at odds with our human experience. The unifying power of the meaning of the divine life expressed as love moving to freedom slips subtly towards conformity to creeds and then yet further into submission to ecclesial institutions, and it all ends up in cultural oppression. Throughout its history the Church has always run the risk, inherent in every institution, of turning what once was liberty and hope for people into demands for conformity. Like the institutions of government it lives with a perpetual struggle for continual renewal against the forces of corruption which turn power so quickly to abusive ends.

The gospel hope

The recognition of the reality of this struggle is the key to its salvation and continued vibrancy in the human story. Diversity is critical to the gospel story. The struggle to accept that the gospel opened its arms to all sides of humanity in the ancient world is a key to understanding the development of the faith in the very early years of the Church. In his dream Peter had to take of that which was unclean and eat (Acts 10:9–23). A struggle was going on inside his soul mirroring the struggle in the mission of the Church as to whether the gospel included all people, Gentiles as well as Jews, on the same basis.

What was happening was not the development of an alternative culture – Christianity alongside Greek or Jewish culture – but the liberation of the cultures of the day in the gospel story. People were not required to stop being Jews when they were baptised or to give up their Greek inheritance but to bring that diversity into the life of the community of faith. Diversity was essential to the integrity of the early Christian communities. It was a struggle. There were forces at work on both sides. There were those who wanted conformity to their history and culture – the circumcision party.

There were those who wanted to turn the Church into a third and alternative culture – the gnostic party. The apostles resisted both diversions. The defining reality of the Church was Jesus Christ risen. They were held together neither by a shared history nor by a desire to set up an alternative culture in this world but by a common and liberating experience of the gospel. So they had to learn to accept one another and minister to one another – a very troublesome and fraught task. They had to learn to help one another interpret the gospel for their own life and culture. Small wonder the early history was full of division and falsity. Every easy option out was cut off from them by the essential vision which had brought them to where they were.

The Church is, therefore, essentially non-sectarian. It may be small and a struggling minority. It may be large and part of an inherited establishment. Whatever its history and circumstance it has to resist sectarianism. It has to both resist the route which would shut its doors to any face of contemporary culture or shut itself off from the world it was seeking to evangelise by trying to create an alternate culture. Many of these challenges represent difficult judgements and very fine lines. An established Church can be sectarian and more so than a tiny minority Church. An established Church runs the temptation of sectarianism by demands for conformity. Non-conformity is a persistent witness to prevent the success of such a strategy. It is a delusion of power to think that the demand for conformity can succeed. As our history reveals even the most repressive of legislative frameworks have never succeeded in making people conform.

If the inner struggle of the Church is always to shape its life in response to the vision of love and freedom in the being of God then the Church can begin to connect with the struggles of our own culture and its political history. There is an essential common ground – the framing of a community of peace in freedom across the range of diversity of our social order. Here we begin to see the interplay of the journey of understanding made in contemporary politics and that made in the community of faith. The meaning takes shape and form in the agreed place Church has in the formal life of the society it serves.

The journey from the centre

Two very important things are happening which affect the political constitution. First, there is an outer movement to recognise the interdependent nature of the world we live in. The idea of the self-sufficient nation state is dead and gone. It was always a myth but it is manifestly untrue now. We depend on the rest of the human community in the world and we express that in the bonds and obligations we accept in the international order.

Second, there is a complementary and paradoxical move away from the centre to the locality. This is happening at all levels of our experience. It is rooted in a growing recognition that different communities not only have different needs but different gifts and skills. Uniform solutions cannot be made to fit the diversity of our life. There has to be devolution from the centre to enable communities which have a conscious sense of identity to exercise greater responsibility for their affairs. This has to happen without destroying the bonds of our shared life in the wider community. Devolution has to avoid sectarianism. It is however inescapable.

It is not just national governments which are having to wrestle with the yielding of power to localities, local government is struggling with the same agenda. There is a growing understanding that different localities within regions have different needs and the task of local political life is to find ways of enabling judgements to be made which accept different solutions in different places. Whilst this is in part driven by an acceptance of the finitude of resources it is also a response to the diversification and flexibility of modern life. Justice and equity can no longer be delivered by giving everyone the same. They have to be worked out in the setting of difference. That is a struggle we are still trying to resolve.

This pattern of life is replicated in other sides of our life beyond the immediate political sphere. Corporate institutions struggle with restructuring aimed at devolving power and responsibility. For some this is a superficial exercise where there has been little understanding of the implications of such cultural shifts for the sharing of power. For others it is a deep and serious change of culture in which the gifts and skills of the people who engage in the task are enabled to affect not only the manner but the content of the work. In the USA there is a small but growing minority of corporate institutions which have gone down the route of including their employees in the core structure of the organisation. All who belong to the enterprise have a stake in the company. United Airlines is a well-known example of this shift to a stakeholder order where power and responsibility are both diffused and shared.

Constitutional change and corporate restructuring are all part of the story of our struggle to make sense of a diversified and flexible world where people are not seeking commonality of outcomes but freedom to develop and flourish.

From local authorities who have devolved their service centres of power and decision-making to localities, to companies who have had the courage to empower their workforces to exercise skilled leadership and innovation, to parliamentary movements to reform the constitution to give a greater sense of direct engagement between people and power – the whole story is one rooted in a common vision and sense of direction. That many do not understand it or resist it in no way undermines the dynamism of the change. This is the front line of struggle with the changing demands of our human life in community today.

The Church cannot escape the shift!

The Church whose history is so closely bound up with the form of our constitution avoids this struggle not only to its own peril but at the risk of losing the opportunity for the gospel to come to the aid of a society in transition. Holding on to the past in effect means being washed up on the beach and left to rot.

Holding on is rooted in fear. Letting go and renegotiating offers hope and a sense of a future contribution. There are particular agendas for the Church of England. They should be of concern to all Christians who need to agree the form of the relationship Christian institutions have to contemporary political and constitutional order. The Church of England's relation to the Crown and Parliament, its system of appointments and the trust it holds in the deployment of its historic resources are all open to fresh debate. The idea that the Prime Minister should exercise some power in the appointment of bishops or that bishops should have an automatic right of entry into Parliament make less and less sense as our society changes and diversifies. The idea that the nation and its representatives take an interest in the well-being of the Church and that the Church, with others, might contribute in forming our social order through the democratic process, is a much more attractive way for the Church and state to relate together today. The willingness to yield outdated privileges rooted in a history long since gone provides the context for the work to be done. It does not predicate the outcome. It does not end the sense of duty held by all Christians to make the gospel story available, by every avenue of service open to it, to the people of this society.

The task, however, belongs to the whole community. What comes out of the process of reflection and revisiting historic agendas must be new agreements and covenants with the people. That is why all Christian Churches and bodies must concern themselves with these things and be ready to make changes within their own culture formed, as part of it has been, in response to an establishment they reject. The change affects us all. If we have to move away from a culture of position and privilege to one of place and service we have likewise to move beyond conformity and non-conformity to communion in our diversity.

The common ground

In thinking this through we should take note that a not too dissimilar journey is happening in the Church as in our politics. We move from the centre in both directions. We move to a greater sense of sharing with the Church across the world. We form new bonds with sister Churches in Europe and in the wider world. And the move is away from centralist strategies for our mission to recognising the need for networking and sustaining the many faces of the Church in local communities and in networks of human experience and culture. We are having to make judgements about strategy in the face of diversity rather than hide behind universal provision or rule books which make no sense of the range of choice and challenge and gift which is our modern life. So we travel the same road as others and we do so as a company whose reason to be is in the vision offered to the world in Jesus Christ. It is at this level that the world of politics and the world of theological and spiritual reflection interconnect. The opportunity is open to us of mutual help through careful listening to what is happening across the range of corporate life. It is a struggle in which mistakes are made, wrong ideas deployed and false paths explored. But it is a journey that cannot be avoided unless we are content to remain dead on the beach, the tide having long since gone out.

14

A Postmodern Church

The Synod of Whitby in 664 brought together the two main traditions of early Christianity in Britain. By these two routes the gospel had been introduced to these islands. Celtic missionaries had spread the Good News across the northern part of Britain and the Roman missionaries, led by Augustine of Canterbury, had evangelised the rest of the country. Two systems were, therefore, living side by side. At the Synod of Whitby decisions were taken about the integration of these two traditions. In terms of order, without questioning the validity of the Celtic tradition, the Synod agreed on the need to accept the Roman structure. From that decision, as the Church became dominant in the culture of Britain and Ireland in the medieval period, the parish system was established providing churches and authorised ministry in every place in the land. The sense of a predominant and universal Christian order created a system which was geared to maintain the Christian inheritance. The sense of a Church moving in mission gave way to a Church sustaining a prevailing culture.

The growing interest, in our own time, in the Celtic tradition both of faith and of spiritual life is indicative of some unease in the Church about the adequacy of the traditional order. The diversity, mobility and changeability of our culture sit ill at ease with the fixed structures of the inherited established order. The Celtic sense of movement, of a spirituality in tune with the basic forces of a living, wonderful and mysterious universe, of simplicity and of minimal structure, appeals to growing numbers of people in our own age as they journey in their own spiritual development.

In parallel fashion the growth of the House Church and

Community Church movement reveals a desire, especially among young people, for more immediacy in spiritual life, for more direct involvement in the ministry of the church, for informality and for less structure. It is the people, meeting in community, not the priest and the building, who form the modern church. In a proper concern for some aspects of the theological thinking of these movements we may well be missing the real issue which has less to do with the detail of theology and much more with the integrity of the experience. That is not to suggest theological issues are not important but rather that, with people who manifestly belong within the mainstream of Christian believing, they should not be the sole focus of what we encounter in these movements.

The growth of movements like Celtic groups, Taizé groups and House and Community Church groups is indicative of a increasing need for different and diverse styles of ministry in the contemporary world. The old order is not meeting the need.

Although these movements are all very diverse and meet different sorts of desire, there are important commonalities. Perhaps the most important is their focus on the journey of faith and the experience of God. It is the essential being of the Christian community which counts. Either the Church is on the journey defined by the vision and experience of God or it is on the road to its grave. It is substance rather than form which matters. So it is not the form of worship nor the style of life which is the focus but the encounter with the heart of all being. A sense of being liberated by a love which endures is the outcome people seek. That enables commitment and commitment sets free for living and for ministry. So the first mark of the postmodern Church is its concern for its core faith – faith being a living encounter of people in community with God. That faith is made particular in the lives of people in diverse communities.

That is what creeds are supposed to be about – a core statement of faith which all can own as the faith which enables people to know and love God. The dynamic of the creeds is exactly what people are seeking in the many ways they make the spiritual journey today – an essential faith which liberates as it opens the door to an encounter with God. Creeds are not twenty impossible things which people who go to traditional Churches have to swallow. They give us a way of articulating our faith and experience in the light of the offering of God for the world in Jesus Christ. So the integration of credal faith with contemporary living faith is essential for the future life of the Church. Simply reciting them will not do. Creeds are there to lead us to God.

The second common point of reference, across the growing diversity of spiritual order today, is a desire for less structure. People want a more direct involvement in the community. Relationships are formed according to the more immediate needs of living. So networking becomes more important than abiding by the formal routes of the structures. The structures have got to have an open and straightforward justification in terms of the ministry now. People simply do not understand why we have to go through some protracted set of procedures before action can happen. Order is needed and recognised but it is people centred rather than procedural. There has to be authority and people to make things happen. But leadership and ministry arise charismatically – according to gift – not out of some long and convoluted process. Time and again people say things like, 'The need is now. If we wait for you to get your act together it will be too late.' The inability of the historic and established Churches to act quickly and respond flexibly drives people to find support and opportunity elsewhere. It is the capacity of the less structured orders to make that more immediate response on the basis of the gifts of the people which makes them pertinent to the emerging needs of our world.

A group of African Christians came to their local priest and said, 'We have been meeting in our village and sharing the gospel with our community over the past year. As a result there are a number of converts to the faith. Can someone come and baptise the new Christians?' The people had got on with the task and now looked to the formal life of the Church to respond to what had happened. Hopefully the priest went not to take over the work but to offer support and wider ministry to encourage them on. The people take the initiative and the Church is a source of help and sustenance.

The third feature in common to these new movements is a sense of flexibility in order and a distinctly non-hierarchical culture. There is an implicit recognition that people bring many different stories to the faith community. By one route or another space has to be given for people to live those stories and find the community of faith a means of help in offering direction for living. Informality provides space and an affirmative non-hierarchical culture enables growth. Informality is not to be equated with the casual. To succeed it requires as much forethought and preparation as formal events. This freer style can collapse into the casual and then it irritates the people and fails to meet the demands of ministry today.

The fourth feature is a clear recognition that experience of church community is about the sustaining of discipleship. It is not an end in itself. There is a holistic desire to integrate faith into the diversity of modern living. The focus of this will be different at different stages of life. It may be the context of education and learning, of youth culture and the club world, the home and the nurture of family, the professional world and the struggles for humanity and decency here, the world of leisure and entertainment, the financial and consumer side of our daily living. There are a multitude of contexts people bring with them and different ones rise to the surface at different moments.

This is why diversity rather than uniformity of styles of ministry is the secret to enabling spiritual growth today. The oneness of the Church – its catholicity – is not about the oneness of the place and the uniform structure of ministry but about the communion that is held together across a multi-faceted response to the needs of people today. The practice of ministry will be in the school, in the home, in the club.

208

That goes alongside the formal life of the Church. We must seek new ways of holding this diversity together in communion. The more relational understanding of ministry which is rooted in Celtic traditions – living in communion with those sent to proclaim the message of the faith – may yet help us in this mobile and multicultural post Christendom world. Such communion will not be about control but about enabling and encouraging.

So the form of Church will focus on core faith, on minimum essential order, on people and their gifts, on flexible patterns of life held together in communion and on a sense of shared community.

There needs to be a dynamic relationship between the business of our human vocation and the worshipping community. What is done in the life of the Church often has echoes back to the ordinary daily life of the community in which the Church was born. The rituals of Church life have their origin in 'secular' living. In many churches, for example, the celebrant of the Eucharist will wash her hands before the thanksgiving. In East Africa a bowl of water, soap and towel are offered to all participants before every meal. Prayers are offered before taking any food and the prayer might be offered by any person who will share in the meal. Thus every meal table is a holy table where guests are made welcome and God is present and thanked for the generous gifts about to be shared in communion with each other. The gathering of the people in the eucharistic life of the church feeds and sustains the eucharistic life of the household.

All life is vocation. Every person needs to fulfil their part if the community is to be fed and sustained. The ministry happens in the fields where the crop is grown, in the home where people are fed and nurtured, in the school where basic learning takes place, in the community where peaceful life is maintained by those who lead. Love in freedom is being worked out in the struggles of vocational life. That happens in the work to make the life of women more bearable as they carry the load of working life in the sustenance of the community. The gospel task is being lived in the context of the daily vocational struggles. The gifts of God belong with all the people and the call to liberate these gifts is the out-working of the ministry of God's Kingdom today. Again, the worshipping and learning life of the Church is there to sustain and nurture these vocations. The symbols of ministry in the Church have to co-relate to the practice of Kingdom ministry in the wider world.

The Church finds that very difficult. The struggle was sym-bolised for me in worship in Africa. At the end of a Mothers Union conference the delegates processed through the town to the church for the final service. There was singing and dancing and celebration. That dancing and singing was carried into the church in a deeply exuberant time of celebration. Suddenly it came to a halt. The clergy procession was ready and from dancing and singing we moved into a Victorian hymn and to the end of the movement of the people. The disjunction between the celebration of the business of our daily life and the worshipping life of the Church is our problem in the West as well. We too do not know how to carry the business of the joys and sorrows, the vocations and their struggles, into the heart of the Church today.

The new movements are, in part, a response to this disjunc-tion. The encouragement is that many are beginning inside and outside the formal structures of the Church to bring these things back into a dynamic and mutually supportive relationship. The domestic meal table and the altar are being brought into a fresh relationship. The struggles for greater love and freedom in our daily vocations need to feed the gifts of ministry and their order in the Church. That is the struggle of our postmodern age. It is the struggle of the Kingdom. The people who are making the journey of faith need setting free for the exercise of their own ministry within the vocations they have to fulfil.

To say this is to build on the work of others. In the middle of the twentieth century Alan Ecclestone sought to move the Church in this direction. His creative and experimental ministry in the Don Valley working-class community of Darnell in Sheffield was rooted in a vision of gospel and Kingdom.[1] The eucharistic life of the local church needed to be expressed in the eucharistic life of the community in which it was set. The formal aspect of Church happened in the two critical and interrelated events of Eucharist on Sunday and the parish meeting midweek. These two things were part of one ministry. For the rest the people took their part in the usual and difficult business of life in the working community of a steel-making parish. The gospel realities were present in all three aspects of the life of the community – in the community meal on Sunday, in the heated debates about the way the gospel responded to the daily issues of living as talked about and debated in the parish meeting, and in the way the church lived its life through its members in the local community. Love working for freedom at all levels.

The visionary ideals of Ecclestone, worked out in Darnall in Sheffield, were quickly dissipated in the Parish Communion Movement which took off in the 1940s onwards. From a movement which integrated vocation and worship, the Church proceeded to think that by focusing on the worship alone it could build community and represent the gospel. It forgot the other side to Ecclestone's vision – the way Eucharist fed the thinking and practice of people as they wrestled with the appalling dilemmas of a heavy industrialised and exploitative society. Getting everyone together around the Holy Table is one face of the gospel. The other is the life the community lives in its many and confusing faces in the world at large.

Ecclestone's world has gone. There can be no return to the solutions struggled with in the heart of an old industrial culture. Visit the Don Valley today and see a new world emerging – a postmodern world of diverse agencies, recreational opportunities, popular culture, consumerism and contemporary corporate enterprise. This world is much more diverse and mobile and disjointed in different ways. The theological theme, however, and value of Ecclestone's work is

211

more long lasting. The dynamic interplay between the different faces of our culture and the journey of faith represented in the life of the worshipping believing community is critical to enabling the gospel to connect with the spiritual quest of our own time. In breaking with the secular Enlightenment themes of modernity and the positivism which arose from it, postmodern people and culture open the way for a recovery of the spiritual.

Creating the Church as a sort of counter-culture to all of this will only serve to drive it deeper into the ghetto and further on to the margins. The possibilities implicit in the gospel encounter, through the people, with the many cultures of our time offer a much more hopeful and open way for future ministry. The silence of God experienced in the face of such confusing plurality leads to a patient listening which, in turn opens the way for the Word of God to be heard again across the full experience of our humanity.

If we accept that the constructs of culture are essentially human – they cannot be absolutised – then the gospel will help people find a way of living in relation to them. Those choices will have to be theirs – sustained by the critical but supportive nurture of all who share the journey of gospel hope. Helping people form their own judgements will be at the heart of the practice of pastoral life. That will be different from trying to get people to conform to a Christianised culture. Instead of saying to people, this is how you must live, we will be saying, this is the vision that leads us on, these are the values which make sense of it, what are the choices which confront you and how can we help you decide?

The critical edge of the gospel to culture is not expressed in offering people another culture – a sort of modern Christendom – but in enabling them to respond where they are. As Richard Niebuhr suggested in his seminal work on Christ and culture there will be moments when the response is welcoming, moments when it is rejecting and many which are 'yes but'.[2] They are decisions, however, which have to be made on the front line of living. So the practice of pastoral work is not in the application of the rule books of the Church but in the living world of faith engaging with the cultures where we have to live day by day. The rule book belongs to the endeavour at providing an abiding Christian culture. Negotiating contemporary culture is more like learning to read a map. It is about helping travellers find the direction. Different conditions may require choosing diverse routes ahead.

Whether it is in the contemplative mood of Taizé or Celtic spirituality or in the exuberant confidence of the alternative Churches the attractiveness is in the outcome for people. They find space for reading the map of their own life and confidence to make decisions about day-to-day living. The new Churches may present as authoritarian but young people who attend them are given confidence to express the faith for themselves and to share in the ministry of the Church. That builds an inner confidence for decisions about living – who to share one's life with, in what direction to move career wise, how to relate to youth culture.

In a different but not unrelated way the growth of contemplative forms of spirituality are about offering people space for their own reflection and for deepening self-awareness as they seek to grow in confidence in the love of God. In a world of activity and many and confusing words there are moments when being and waiting provide the chance to gain fresh and liberating perspective on the choices to be made.

So if the form of the Church is to be focused on core vision and faith, on minimum flexible transparent order and on inclusive non hierarchical cultures, its dynamic will focus on worship, learning, contemplation, and mutual support and sustenance. All will be implicitly directed towards the living encounter of the gospel story with our many stories.

The business of worship, learning, contemplation and mutual support must shape the contemporary form of the Church. I will illustrate the difficulty we have in this shift of culture by considering some of the problems and questions which the Church of England has struggled with. The debate about who should preside at the Eucharist is a case in point. The temptation of the old culture is to find cogent reasons why only ordained priests may preside. The demand of the new culture, however, is to begin with the celebration of the whole community. The Holy Meal is something we make together. The roles which different people have in making it happen cannot be separated from the common life of the whole company. All are guests, all are servants of the others and all are invited to share in the meal. Then we can ask how people can be given roles so that the meal happens with a sense of occasion, mystery and delight. The old order says, 'Only the priest can do it.' The new says, 'Will you be our minister and enable this meal to take place?' The first threatens to be both hierarchical and exclusive. The latter inclusive and orderly. Someone has to be set aside to hold the bowl and the towel so that all may participate in the meal.[3]

Or to take another matter which will soon arise among us – the way we conduct our ordinations to ministry. Having conducted ordinations to the priesthood and shared in consecrations of bishops according to the rites of the Church of England I am conscious of the excluding character of aspects of the liturgy. A great scrum of (all male) bishops envelopes the new bishop at the laying on of hands. In like manner a great cloud of priestly witnesses descends on the person being ordained priest. The ritual gives little sense that such ministry arises out of the whole Church – that it is rooted in the life of the people of God (the *laos* to which all of us belong). It runs the risk of being a moment seen as exclusion rather than celebration.

These larger issues are reflected in the life of the Church as a whole: the releasing of people for worship, the encouragement of people to learn together, the enabling of a wide and varied set of vocations and the constant interplay of the many different lives people live with the mystery of faith.

The way we do things and the symbols we create are critical

to our capacity to engage with the emerging cultures of our world.

We have a choice: defend the inheritance as we have received it or reshape and redefine our understanding and role. These mobile and open times offer us an unparalleled opportunity, if with courage we are prepared to reform ourselves, to connect with the dynamic of love working for freedom and to share in the mystery of the liberating love of God.

Notes

Introduction

1. John Updike, *In the Beauty of the Lilies* (Penguin, 1996), p. 5.
2. John 4:1–42.
3. See Luke 20:20–47.
4. Luke 10:29–37.
5. Luke 10:38–42.
6. The changes in European culture at the end of the seventeenth century are discussed in Herbert Butterfield, *Christianity in European History* (Collins, 1952), pp. 35ff. Butterfield notes both the detachment of thought from religion and Christian justifications and also the emerging of the scientific age of Enlightenment with its offer of hope of progress in human affairs.
7. It has been suggested that the Byzantine design of the Dome of the Rock indicates a significant Christian contribution to its construction.
8. V. Havel, speech at Aachen, May 1996, as reported in the *New York Review of Books*, June 1996, and quoted by J. Gladwin in 'Of Fish and Altars' in *Anvil*, vol. 13, no. 3, 1996.

CHAPTER 1: The Silence of God

1. See F. Nietzsche, *The Twilight of the Idols*, vol. 12 of *Works*, ed. O. Levy (English version, Allen and Unwin, 1909–13) and *The Will to Power*, vol. 2 of *Works* and vol. 16 *The Antichrist*, p. 16. God is 'a declaration of hostility towards life, nature, the will to life ... It is the will to nothingness sanctified', quoted in A.C. Thistleton, *Interpreting God and the Postmodern Self* (T & T Clarke, 1995), p. 125.
2. J.B. Metz, 'Facing the Jews' in J.B. Metz and J. Moltmann, *Faith and the Future* (Orbis, 1995), pp. 38ff.
3. The two secular and contrasting attempts at producing a secular philosophical justification for freedom are: J. Rawls, *A Theory of*

Justice (Belknap, 1971); R. Nozick, *Anarchy, State and Utopia* (Basic Books, 1974).

4. Karl Barth, *The Epistle to the Romans* (OUP, 1933, translated from the 1921 edition by Edward C. Hoskyns). This is the classic text which gave such impetus to the Biblical Theology movement and the recovery of existential theology in the twentieth century. It was pivotal to the Protestant resistance of fascism which was seen as a blasphemous idolatry.

5. P.T. Forsyth, *The Justification of God* (Independent Press, 1957); *The Work of Christ* (Collins, 1965); *The Church, the Gospel and Society* (Independent Press, 1962).

6. R. Niebuhr, *Moral Man and Immoral Society* (Charles Scribner, 1932).

7. Key examples of the range of liberation theology are evidenced in: G. Gutiérrez, *A Theology of Liberation* (Orbis, 1973); J. Bonino, *Revolutionary Theology Comes of Age* (SPCK, 1975); J. Secundo, *Grace and the Human Condition* (Orbis, 1973).

8. J. Secundo, *The Community called Church* (Orbis, 1972).

9. See F. Nietzsche, *The Gay Science* (Vintage Books, 1974). For a discussion of this see G. Cutting (ed.), *The Cambridge Companion to Michael Foucault* (Cambridge University Press, 1994), p. 132, where there is a comment on Nietzsche in the setting of Foucault's interest in issues to do with the *melete thanaton* – classic meditations on death.

CHAPTER 2: God and the Meaning of Freedom

1. M. Luther, *The Bondage of the Will*, tr. J.I. Packer and A.R. Johnston (James Clarke, 1957). This is Luther's response to Erasmus' *The freedom of the Will* (*Lugundi Betavorum* (IX), reprinted, 1963).

2. Calvin emphasised the freedom and sovereignty of the Divine Will. This is discussed in F. Wendel, *Calvin* (Fontana, 1965), pp. 177ff.

3. E.P. Thompson, *The Making of the English Working Class* (Pelican Books, 1968). Pages 45–8 discuss the relationship of Methodism to the development of labour unions.

4. See James Cone, *God of the Oppressed* (Seabury Press, 1975).

5. Ebelard Bethge, *Dietrich Bonhoeffer* (New York, 1975).

6. S. Hawking, *A Brief History of Time* (Bantam Press, 1988).

7. R. Dawkins, *The Selfish Gene* (OUP, 1976); *The Extended Phenotype* (W.H. Freeman, 1982).

8. Hawking, *A Brief History of Time*, p. 175.

9. M. Foucault, *Madness and Civilisation*, translated from the French

by R. Howard (Routledge, 1971), originally published as *Histoire de la Folie*.

10. G. Cutting, (ed.), *The Cambridge Companion to Michael Foucault* (Cambridge University Press, 1994), p. 54.

11. See, for example, Peter Hodgson, *Winds of the Spirit – A Constructive Christian Theology* (SCM, 1994).

CHAPTER 3: Creation and the Meaning of Freedom

1. See J.T. McNeill, *The History and Character of Calvinism* (Oxford University Press, 1967), pp. 210ff.

2. S. Hawking, *A Brief History of Time* (Bantam Press, 1988).

3. An example of this approach is John Owen, *Death of Death in the Death of Jesus Christ* (first published 1648 and republished by Banner of Truth Trust 1959).

4. R. Dawkins, *The Selfish Gene* (Oxford University Press, 1976); *The Extended Phenotype* (W.H. Freeman, 1982).

5. A full exposition of a theological interpretation and response to the contemporary scientific debate is to be found in A. Peacocke, *Theology for a Scientific Age* (SCM, 1990).

6. On the subject of freedom in creation see Ruth Page, *God and the Web of Creation* (SCM, 1997).

7. Page, *God and the Web of Creation*.

8. M. Polanyi, *Personal Knowledge* (Routledge, Kegan and Paul, 1958) makes a powerful statement to the interaction of the personal with the material world and the task of science.

CHAPTER 4: The Holy Trinity and the Meaning of Autonomy and Community

1. K.R. Popper, *The Open Society and its Enemies* (Routledge, 1945).

2. F.A. Hayek, *The Constitution of Liberty* (Routledge, Kegan and Paul, 1960).

3. R. Nozick, *Anarchy, State and Utopia* (Basic Books, 1974).

4. J. Locke, 'An Essay Concerning the True Original, Extent and End of Civil Government' in *Social Contract*, introduction by Sir Ernest Baker (OUP, 1947) and Thomas Hobbes, *Leviathan* (republished J.M. Dent, 1914).

CHAPTER 5: Jerusalem – Nightmare or Vision

1. Koran, translated by N.J. Dawood (Penguin, 1956).

2. SABEEL is a Christian Palestinian Liberation Theology Centre in

Jerusalem committed to research the meaning of justice and peace for the peoples of the Holy Land.
3. For a brief but excellent insight into secular Zionism see Norman Cantor, *The Sacred Chain. A History of the Jews* (Fontana, 1996), pp. 288–300.

For a discussion of Western Fundamentalism and Zionism see Dan Wagner, 'Marching to Zion – Western Evangelicals and Jerusalem approaching the Year 2000' in *Jerusalem – What Makes for Peace?* ed. N. Ateek, C. Duaybis and M. Schoder (Melisende, 1997).
4. Theodore Herzl was the critical leader and philosopher of Zionism. See Herzl, *The Old New Land*, translated by Lotte Levensholm (Hertzl Publishing, 1960).
5. J. Esquito, 'Christian Muslim Relations in Historic Perspective' in Ateek, Duaybis and Schoder, *Jerusalem – What Makes for Peace?*

CHAPTER 6: The European Question

1. *New York Review of Books*, 1996.
2. See Alan Wilkinson, *The Church of England and the First World War* (SPCK, 1978); *Dissent or Conform* (SCM, 1986).
3. The two-volume *History of the Ecumenical Movement* is a vital resource: *Volume 1*, ed. Ruth Rouse and Stephen Neill (published by SPCK, 1956 and now WCC); Volume 2 (on the post 1948 material) ed. Harold Fry (SPCK, 1970, now published by WCC).

CHAPTER 7: The Pre-Modern Moving to the Postmodern World

1. On Human Rights see S. Bailey, *Human Rights and Responsibilities in Britain and Ireland* (MacMillan, 1988).
2. Sarah Nelson, *Ulster's Uncertain Defenders* (Appletree, 1984).
3. On Edmund Burke and Ireland as an example of the beginning of the nineteenth-century debate over Ireland see Connor Cruise O'Brien, *The Great Melody* (Minerva, 1992), pp. 1–86.
4. See O. Chadwick, *The Victorian Church* Part 2 (A & C Black, 1970), pp. 427–39.
5. See F. Wright, *Northern Ireland – a Comparative Analysis* (Gill and MacMillan, 1987).
6. R. Eames, *Chains to be Broken* (Weidenfeld and Nicolson, 1992).

CHAPTER 8: The Meaning of Community

1. Geoff Mulgan, *Politics in an Antipolitical Age* (Polity Press, 1994). This book examines the significance of the shifts of political culture in the last decades of the twentieth century and what this means

for the organisation and culture of politics as it enters the twenty-first century.
2. Reinhold Niebuhr, *Moral Man and Immoral Society* (Charles Scribner, 1932).
3. Reinhold Niebuhr, *Children of Light and Children of Darkness* (Charles Scribner's Sons, 1944).
4. Mulgan, *Politics in an Antipolitical Age*, p. 69: 'despite unprecedented prosperity and technological control, the late twentieth century has been characterised by an unmistakeable undercurrent of doubt and fear. This uncertain spirit is reflected in the cultural theories of postmodernism, which calls into question the very idea of a single truth and a single reading of the world . . . with unpredictable change comes endemic uncertainty, about everything from culture to truth, to the climate, the air we breathe and the skills we learn . . .'

CHAPTER 9: Life in the Home

1. Sir William Beveridge, *Social Insurance and Allied Services* (HMSO, 1942).
2. Pat Barker, *Regeneration* (Viking, 1991); *Eye in the Door* (Viking, 1993); *The Ghost Road* (Viking, 1995).
3. Karl Barth, *Church Dogmatics* Vol. 111: 4, p. 454: 'Does not war demand that almost everything God has forbidden be done on a broad front?'
4. *Putting Asunder* – a *Divorce Law for Contemporary Society*, Report of the Commission of the Archbishop of Canterbury (SPCK, 1966).
5. These and other statistics in this chapter are in *Social Focus on Families* (HMSO, 1997).
6. *Social Focus on Families.*
7. For example, *The Family in Contemporary Society*, Report for the Lambeth Conference (SPCK, 1958).
8. References in *The Family in Contemporary Society* to Resolutions of the Lambeth Conference 1908 (Resolutions 41, 43), Lambeth Conference 1920 (Resolution 68) and Lambeth 1930 (Resolution 15).

CHAPTER 10: Art and the Meaning of Prophecy in the Twentieth Century

1. See Picasso's 'Les Demoiselles d'Avignon', Museum of Modern Art in New York.
2. There is an interesting discussion of the significance of Picasso in

H.R. Rookmaaker, *Modern Art and the Death of a Culture* (IVP, 1970), pp. 113–122.
3. Salman Rushdie, *Satanic Verses* (The Consortium, 1992).
4. A. Camus, *La Peste* (1947).
5. Some of Shostakovich's great symphonies were composed during the 1930s' Stalinist terror.
6. Ebelard Bethge, *Dietrich Bonhoeffer* (New York, 1975).

CHAPTER 11: Media – the Virtual Reality of our Time

1. David Daniell, *William Tyndale – a biography* (Yale, 1994).
2. David Daniell, *Tyndale's New Testament* (Yale, 1989), p. xxix.

CHAPTER 12: The Church

1. See *Book of Common Prayer* (OUP), Article 19.
2. D. Cupitt, *Sea of Faith* (CUP 1988).
3. See E. Halevy, *History of the English People in the Nineteenth Century* Vol. 1 1815 (Ernest Benn Ltd, 1924), Part 111, Chapter 1, pp. 387ff.

CHAPTER 13: Changing the Establishment for the Good of the Nation

1. *The Brixton Disorders* (HMSO Comnd 8427, 1981).
2. See A.D. Gilbert, *Religion and Society in Industrial England* (Longman, 1976), pp. 125ff. and 162ff.

CHAPTER 14: A Postmodern Church

1. Tim Gorringe, *Alan Ecclestone* (Sheffield Cairns Publications, 1994).
2. H.R. Niebuhr, *Christ and Culture* (Faber and Faber, 1952).
3. See *Eucharistic Presidency*, Report of the House of Bishops (CHP, 1997).

Bibliography

Postmodernism and social theory and theology

Adam, A.K.M., *What is Postmodernist Biblical Criticism?* (Fortress Press, 1995)

Clarke, David, *Changing World, Unchanging Church* (Mowbray, 1997)

Davie, G., *Religion in Britain since 1945* (Blackwell, 1994)

Gill, R., *Theology and Sociology* (Cassell, 1997), especially pp. 429ff.

Lakeland, Paul, *Christian Identity in a Fragmented Age* (Fortress Press, 1997)

Middleton, J. Richard and Walsh, Brian J., *Truth is Stranger than It Used to Be* (SPCK, 1995)

Millbank, J., *Theology and Social Theory* (Blackwell, 1990)

Mulgan, G., *Politics in an Antipolitical Age* (Polity Press, 1994)

Thistleton, A.C., *Interpreting God and the Postmodern Self* (T & T Clarke, 1995)

Philosophy and Social Theory

Cutting, G. (ed.), *The Cambridge Companion to Michael Foucault* (Cambridge, 1994)

Foucault, M., *Madness and Civilisation* (Routledge, 1971, originally published in French *Histoire de la Folie*)

Hayek, F.A., *The Constitution of Liberty* (Routledge, Kegan and Paul, 1960)

Hobbes, Thomas, *Leviathan* (J.M. Dent, 1914)

Locke, J., 'An Essay Concerning the true Original, Extent and End of Civil Government' in *Social Contract*, introduced by Sir Ernest Baker (OUP, 1947)

Niebuhr, R., *Moral Man and Immoral Society* (Charles Scribner, 1932)

Nietzsche, F., *The Will to Power*, Vol. 2 of *Works*, ed. O. Levy (Allen and Unwin, 1909–13)

The Gay Science (Vintage Books, 1974)

Nozick, R., *Anarchy, State and Utopia* (Basic Books, 1974)

Polanyi, M., *Personal Knowledge* (Routledge, Kegan and Paul, 1958)

Popper, K.R., *The Open Society and its Enemies* (Routledge, 1945)
Rawls, J., *A Theory of Justice* (Belknap, 1971)

Theology

Barth, K., *The Epistle to the Romans* (OUP, 1933)
Bonino, J., *Revolutionary Theology Comes of Age* (SPCK, 1975)
Bowker, J., *Is God a Virus?* (SPCK, 1995)
Cone, J., *A Black Theology of Liberation* (Lippincott, 1970)
Forsyth, P.T., *The Church, the Gospel and Society* (Independent Press, 1962)
Gutiérrez, G., *A Theology of Liberation* (Orbis, 1973)
Hodgson, P., *Winds of the Spirit* (SCM, 1994)
Leech, K., *The Sky is Red* (Darton, Longman & Todd, 1997)
Metz, J.B. and Moltmann, J., *Faith and the Future* (Orbis, 1995)
Moltmann, J., *God in Creation* (SCM, 1985)
Page, R., *God and the Web of Creation* (SCM, 1997)
Peacocke, A., *Theology for a Scientific Age* (SCM, 1990)
Ward, K., *God, Chance and Necessity* (Oneworld, 1996)
Wright, N.T., *Jesus and the Victory of God* (SPCK, 1996)

History

Bethge, E., *Dietrich Bonhoeffer* (New York, 1975)
Butterfield, H., *Christianity in European History* (Collins, 1952)
Chadwick, O., *The Secularisation of the European Mind in the 19th Century* (CUP, 1975)
Cragg, K., *The Arab Christian – a History of the Middle East* (Mowbray, 1992)
Daniel, D., *William Tyndale* (Yale, 1994)
Foucault, M., *The History of Sexuality* (Penguin, 1984)
Fry, H. (ed.), *The History of the Ecumenical Movement* Vol. 2 (SPCK and WCC, 1970)
Gilbert, A.D., *Religion and Society in Industrial England* (Longman, 1976)
Gillis, J.R., *For Better For Worse – British Marriages since 1600* (Oxford, 1985)
Gorringe, T., *Alan Ecclestone* (Sheffield Cairns Publications, 1994)
McNeill, J.T., *The History and Character of Calvinism* (Oxford University Press, 1967)
O'Brien, C.C., *The Great Melody* (Minerva, 1992)
Rouse, Ruth and Neill, Stephen (eds.), *The History of the Ecumenical Movement* Vol. 1 (SPCK and WCC, 1956)

Thompson, E.P., *The Making of the English Working Class* (Pelican, 1968)

Wendel, F., *Calvin* (Fontana, 1965)

Wilkinson, A., *The Church of England and the First World War* (SPCK, 1978)
Dissent or Conform (SCM, 1986)

Culture, Art and Media

Arnason, H.H., *A History of Modern Art* (Thames and Hudson, 1969)

Chardin, Teilhard de, *The Future of Man* (Fontana, 1969)

Glasgow Media Group, *Bad News* (RKP, 1976)

Lovgren, S., *The Genesis of Modernism* (Stockholm, 1959)

McKinney, R.W.A. (ed.), *Creation, Christ and Culture* (essays in honour of T.F. Torrance) (T & T Clarke, 1976)

Newbigin, L., *The Gospel in a Pluralist Society* (SPCK, 1989)

Niebuhr, H.R., *The Nature and Destiny of Man* (Scribners, 1943)
Radical Monotheism and Western Culture (Harper, 1943)
Christ and Culture (Faber & Faber, 1952)

Porter, D., *The Word on the Box* (Paternoster, 1997)

Rookmaaker, H.R., *Modern Art and the Death of a Culture* (IVP, 1970)

Tillich, P., *Theology of Culture* (New York, 1959)

Issues and Public Reports

Ateek, N., Duaybis, C. and Schoder, M., *Jerusalem – What Makes for Peace?* (Melisende, 1997)

Bailey, S., *Human Rights and Responsibilities in Britain and Ireland* (MacMillan, 1988)

Beveridge, W., *Social Insurance and Allied Services* (HMSO, 1942)

Brixton Disorders (HMSO, 1981)

Cantor, N., *The Sacred Chain. A History of the Jews* (Fontana, 1996)

Dawkins, R., *The Selfish Gene* (OUP, 1976)
The Extended Phenotype (W.H. Freeman, 1982)

Eames, R., *Chains to be Broken* (Weidenfeld and Nicolson, 1992)

Family in Contemporary Society, Report for the Lambeth Conference (SPCK, 1958)

Hawking, S., *A Brief History of Time* (Bantam Press, 1988)

Nazir-Ali, M., *Islam. A Christian Perspective* (Paternoster, 1983)

Nelson, S., *Ulster's Uncertain Defenders* (Appletree, 1984)

Putting Asunder – a Divorce Law for Contemporary Society, Report of the Commission of the Archbishop of Canterbury, (SPCK, 1966)

Social Focus on Families (HMSO, 1997)

Social Justice, Report of the Commission on Social Justice (IPPR, 1994)

Wright, F., *Northern Ireland – a Comparative Analysis* (Gill and Mac-Millan, 1987)

Index